HOPE BEYOND REHAB

A GUIDE TO UNDERSTANDING AND HELPING THE ADDICT YOU LOVE

CHARLES CAMORATA

CONTENTS

Dedication   vii
Introduction   ix

1. MY JOURNEY   1
   A Most Unique Opportunity   3
   In The Trenches   4

2. THINGS ARE NOT ALWAYS AS THEY SEEM   8
   The Root   9

3. REALITY VS. FANTASY   12
   Not Just Drugs Or Alcohol   15
   The Path Of Destruction   16

4. DENIAL   18
   Addiction Cannot Be Legislated   21
   Not Just An Addict's Problem   22

5. THE ADDICT   27
   A Spiritual Issue   29
   What To Do   31

6. A WORLD OF ITS OWN   34
   What Are They Thinking   35
   I Only Smoke Weed   37
   Not For Everyone   39
   The Nurse's Daughter   41
   Do Not Judge   43

7. LATE-STAGE ALCOHOLISM   45
   Tough Times   48
   Be Honest With Yourself   53

8. FAMILIES   55
   Widows And Orphans   57
   The Breakdown   59
   Seek The Lord   61
   Working Together   63
   A Note To Fathers   66

9. CHOOSING A RECOVERY PATH	69
Short-Term & Outpatient Treatment	71
Short-Term Solutions	72
New Beginnings	74
Secular Recovery Programs	75
Faith-Based Recovery Programs	76
Combination Recovery Programs	76
Twelve Steps	77
Christian Recovery Programs	80
Counseling	82
The Stronghold Of Recovery	84
10. RELAPSE PREVENTION	87
What If It Happens	91
11. REGENERATION: THE HOPE BEYOND REHAB	93
Regeneration	95
12. DRUG INFORMATION	98
Marijuana	100
Synthetic Marijuana	102
Medical Marijuana	104
Ecstasy	105
Flakka	106
Prescription Medications	107
Heroin	109
Fentanyl	110
Cocaine	111
Meth (Methamphetamines)	113
Anti-Drug Drugs	114
A Final Word	116
13. BEFORE YOU GO	118
About the Author	119

Hope Beyond Rehab

A Guide to Understanding and Helping the Addict You Love

Copyright © 2023 by Charles A. Camorata

All rights reserved.
No parts of this book may be copied, distributed, or published in any form without permission from the publisher.
For permissions contact: RyKrisLLC@gmail.com.

The names and identifying details of many individuals in this book have been changed. Any resemblance to actual people or personal situations is entirely coincidental.

This book contains the opinions of the author gained through personal experience and reports from recovering addicts as related to drug and alcohol addiction recovery. It is not meant to replace your physician, psychiatrist, or licensed psychologist.
The publisher and the author disclaim liability for any medical or psychological outcomes that may occur as a result of applying any information or suggestions of this book.

eBook ISBN: 978-1-7344507-1-2
Paperback ISBN: 978-1-7344507-0-5
Library of Congress Control Number: 2023905170
Cover design by Kirsten Aufhammer
Edited by Diane Neff-Blackton

All Scripture quotations, unless otherwise indicated, are taken from the Holy Bible, New International Version®, NIV®. Copyright ©1973, 1978, 1984, 2011 by Biblica, Inc.® Used by permission of Zondervan. All rights reserved worldwide. www.zondervan.com The "NIV" and "New International Version" are trademarks registered in the United States Patent and Trademark Office by Biblica, Inc.®

Scripture quotations taken from the (NASB®) New American Standard Bible®, Copyright © 1960, 1971, 1977, 1995 by The Lockman Foundation. Used by permission. All rights reserved. www.lockman.org

Published by: RyKris Publishing, 1603 Capitol Ave. Ste. 310 A522, Cheyenne, WY. 82001

❦ Created with Vellum

DEDICATION

*This book is dedicated to the memory of
my dear friend and brother in Christ*

Joshua Conrad

INTRODUCTION

Addiction has become one of the most serious societal issues of our time. It is killing our children at an alarming and steadily increasing rate. It is also the driving force behind an ever-increasing amount of criminal activity. But it's more than just a societal issue; it's a personal and family issue as well. It's hard to find a single soul who has not been affected by some sort of addiction somewhere within their extended family. It has affected almost every classroom, business, sport, and congregation in the country.

People struggle with addictions to drugs, alcohol, sex, pornography, gambling, eating, internet surfing, texting, exercising, video games, and other compulsive behaviors, and are lost, unable, or unwilling to come to terms with their personal truths. Addiction is a very misunderstood affliction, with a wide range of opinions regarding its root causes, as well as the most effective recovery process. Some opinions are based on reality while the majority of the others are based on hearsay, assumptions, and fear.

Just because someone has struggled with an addiction and went through a personal recovery process doesn't mean they automatically have a true understanding of the big picture. They

Introduction

may have an acute understanding of their own struggle and maybe the experiences of a few other people they've come to know through their own journey, but there's much more to it than what can be learned by simply going through a personal experience.

Some believe that addiction is solely a medical or psychological issue. I have reviewed countless studies and statistics regarding success rates for different recovery methods, reasons for addictions to different substances and activities, relapse rates, you name it. I have found these studies to be of limited use at best due to the nature of addiction itself. What makes many of these studies immaterial is that most addicts become masters at manipulation, lying, deceiving, and denying their addiction. These traits become deeply embedded in the minds and behaviors of addicts, if for no other reason than survival in their addiction. I've known addicts who have broken one of their own bones or knocked out a tooth so they can be prescribed pain medication. This makes the validity of studies based on questionnaires and personal histories highly suspect. For these reasons, I believe the Lord has led me to compile the information in this book in a different way. One that He has laid out for me, and now for you.

For twenty-five years, before entering recovery, I was a functional alcoholic in the music and entertainment industry, where substance abuse was not taken very seriously until just recently. Even today it's really no surprise when someone in the entertainment industry checks themselves into rehab. In fact, instead of being stigmatized as one might expect their popularity in many cases increases.

During my pre-recovery years, I worked and traveled with many other performers who could not function without some substance in their systems daily. Although they would be so messed up they could barely tie their own shoes, at show time they could sing and play their instruments with amazing proficiency, showing no signs of their condition. Because of those

Introduction

experiences I was never really convinced that I had a serious problem.

Twice, I attended twelve-step meetings for more than a year, even participating in a nine-month outpatient recovery program. Through all those efforts, I convinced myself I was no different than most people who drank after work and at parties because I was still able to show up for work. I performed my job well whether playing the piano, writing and producing music for my own recording group as well as other artists, producing music for corporate clients, consulting for large entertainment companies, or even running an international recording and entertainment company. But then one day it all came crashing down. The only place it looked like I could turn to get help was a residential recovery program. It was there that the Lord began to reveal His plans for me.

It has been more than sixteen years since I entered that program. The first year I spent recovering, learning, and realigning my life with God's will. Since then, I've spent the entire time living with recovering addicts 24/7 to minister, teach, and encourage those who were struggling in the grips of addiction as I had, and even worse. I was finally able to slow down long enough to hear the Lord's voice and make a choice of whether I was going to obey it or just continue in my life, only without alcohol. I chose to listen to the Lord and stay in Recovery Ministry. Since 2007 I have been working with men in addiction, helping them change their lives through acceptance of and obedience to Jesus Christ. I've gotten to intimately know them through counseling, praying with them, hoping with them, worshiping with them, fellowshipping with them, and overseeing them. Since I live in the same community, I can observe them every day. This enables me to compare their view of themselves with what they demonstrate through the daily behavior I've witnessed.

I believe the Lord has asked me to write this book. For more than five years I've known that this is what I was being asked to

Introduction

do, but the time did not feel right until now. There is a lot of ground covered in these pages. I've written each chapter to stand on its own as much as possible, so it's not necessary to have read the previous chapters to understand any one of them. Some could easily be expanded into books of their own. My goal, however, is to give you an overview of addiction and its possible root causes, along with an avenue to pursue in getting the help you may need, whether you are an addict yourself or one who has a friend or loved one that needs help.

There is freedom from addiction through Christ. Some are healed and delivered the moment they accept Christ as their Lord and Savior. Some, like me, have been saved at some point in their lives but have drifted far enough away to fall prey to their addictive nature, and some still need to seek and find Christ for the first time. Whatever your situation, God has given us the answer through His Son. I pray that you find the answers you may be looking for in these pages, but more importantly, that you become a disciple of our Lord Jesus Christ experiencing the love and comfort of His Holy Spirit.

Yours in Christ,
    Charlie Camorata

1

MY JOURNEY

What is addiction and how can we treat it, control it, or eliminate it? This is a compelling question. In recent years, society has only begun to realize how serious the problem is, not only for those directly affected by it, but for society as a whole. I've spent over a decade of my life living and working in a community of recovering addicts. Twenty-four hours a day, seven days a week, I'm with people who have been addicted to drugs or alcohol at some time in their lives. It is a men's Christian regeneration program designed to help anyone who has come to the end of their rope because of drugs and/or alcohol addiction and who truly want to change. My time here began as a result of a car accident and a DUI. Sadly, it was not my first.

I wasn't what most people think of when picturing an alcoholic or drug addict. I was the president of an international company, and what is commonly referred to as a "functional" alcoholic. I was married but separated, with two beautiful children, attended church regularly and played piano in several praise bands. From the outside it appeared that I was leading a successful and fulfilling life, (with the exception of my marriage) but I was actually dying on the inside. Everything came crashing down after the accident, not because of any injury, but because I had lost everything that meant anything to me. At the time of the accident, I had already been separated from my family for six years, but the DUI certainly added to their disappointment and shame, and consequently added to my guilt. The day after the accident I was asked to resign by the Board of Directors, something I never considered could happen. I suppose I thought that because of my position something like that would not even be considered, much less occur. Because of these events, it was painfully obvious that something had to change or there was really no reason for my existence. It was not until I had lost everything that I decided to make a change, regardless of what it would take. For me it meant finding a recovery program and coming to terms with myself. I had no idea where it would lead me.

Entering a rehabilitation program was not the beginning of my experience with addicts and alcoholics. As a professional musician and later as a composer, producer, and record company executive, I was in close association with addicts and alcoholics for many years. Performing in concerts, dinner theaters, lounges, and bars also put me in the company of many people under the influence. Just about every adult has had those encounters, however, since it was also my work environment, I experienced it every day. But it was not those chance meetings in a club or party atmosphere that revealed the real picture to me. It was through many of the people with whom I had closely worked.

Over those 25 years, I became close friends with some of my fellow musicians and clients, getting to know their families as well. I was close enough with many of them to know and sometimes understand why they were addicts but didn't pay much attention to it at the time. Not until much later, while I was in a recovery program myself, did I realize how significant those experiences were in the big picture of my life. My road to recovery was rocky and uncharted. I've been in out-patient programs, professional counseling, and was diagnosed with bipolar disorder for which I took medication for years, all of which are no longer necessary.

Today I'm pastor and director of the same program the Lord provided to save my life. It's a nine-month Christ-based recovery program that has been helping men change their lives for more than thirty-eight years. The program's founder, Father Michael Grenier, has dedicated his life to providing food, clothing, shelter, counseling, and teaching for men struggling with addiction. He has done all of this through his submission to Jesus Christ and guidance from the Holy Spirit. He was trained in a similar program that has been doing the same thing for more than sixty years. I've provided contact information for both programs at the end of this book.

Through these teachings and experiences, God has turned all the negative, life-destroying anguish in my life into something I never could have imagined. I am now able to help others in their journeys of learning how to live a life free of addiction, in part due to my experiences during those years. I say in part because I know that it was God's providence that enabled me to process all that I have been through in a way that can be passed on to others.

A Most Unique Opportunity

I've had the unique opportunity to study and learn about addiction, the addict, the addicts' families, and all aspects surrounding their lives by living where they live. I've also studied at length about chemical dependence, inner healing, socioeconomics, addictive personalities, co-dependence, psychology, counseling, and anything else I could find that even remotely related to addiction in addition to Bible study, seminary, and other studies required for my pastoral vocation. It's probably safe to say that the experiences I've had would not have likely happened had I become a psychologist or psychiatrist working in the addiction field.

It's frowned upon for such medical professionals to have personal relationships with their patients. Even if they wanted to spend more personal time with the people they treat, they could not because of the tight guidelines they must adhere to in order to comply with the law and retain their licenses. Consequently, most of their knowledge about addiction depends on classroom education, studying reports, and participating or reviewing clinical and non-clinical studies with only short periods of personal interaction with multiple patients.

Clinical and non-clinical studies are a common source of misinformation because they typically examine a cross-section of people from dissimilar backgrounds and different addictions in the same study. There are also time gaps between when the subjects are asked specific questions and when they record or report their feelings and behaviors. Therefore, the accuracy of many such studies relies on the memory, perspective and the honesty of the people filling out the questionnaires or reporting during sessions. There is an inherent flaw in attempting to study human behavior in this manner. Without constant supervision and oversight, the data gathering is ultimately left to an addicted or recovering subject's individual accountability.

In The Trenches

As I mentioned earlier, I've lived and worked beside people in recovery and have overseen a constantly changing community of individuals at "rock bottom." I've associated with both the addicts and their loved ones and have repeatedly seen their heart-wrenching struggle to lead productive lives. The community provided me the opportunity to interact with people in different stages of recovery, as well as some who have just begun to seek freedom from drug and/or alcohol addiction. I'm currently the pastor of the church in that community, but that has not always been the case. What has not changed over all these years is that even though each day is different, it is ultimately the same. Addiction, and its life-altering results, has not changed. It has only gotten worse, as is the case with any evil that is not confronted and defeated through Christ.

The program I oversee has 40 beds, although at times we have had almost 60. Men ages 20 to 60+ come to us from diverse situations: from jail, prison, homelessness, at the insistence of loved ones, you name it, but all have come to realize their brokenness. Some have jobs and places to live when they reach out for help with the hope of changing things before everything is lost. Some have already lost everything. Some are divorced, some married, some with children and some who have never married. We've had men in their forties who have never lived outside of their parents' home and some who have not lived with their families since childhood. Some have been abused sexually, emotionally, and/or physically, and some have had what appears from the outside, an ideal family and upbringing. Addicts come from every walk of life, and I have seen many of them, including business owners, computer programmers, accountants, pastors, pastors' children, airline pilots, stockbrokers, real estate agents, mechanics, landscapers, painters, deacons, skilled professionals, and unskilled laborers. One thing is the same for all of them: they are all desperate. They may not know how to handle that desperation, but they know something must change.

I make it a point to talk with each person regularly while they are in the program, and I can assure you each one has a different story and different issues that contributed to their addiction. During each person's stay, I spend quite a bit of time talking with them to learn how they view themselves in the world around them. I have the opportunity to observe their behavior, listen to their tone of voice while watching how they carry themselves at different times of the day and from one day to the next. I see how they interact with others in every kind of daily situation from rising in the morning, to eating meals together, to working together, to spending leisure time together, during playtime, alone time, and nearly every aspect of life. In many cases I'm fortunate enough to get to know, or at least talk with their parents, spouses, children, or others close to them. This enables me to compare what close relations say about the individual and his life, comparing it to what he has told me. It's been incredibly valuable to observe the different perspectives and see how various people interpret the same situations.

Over the years I've had this kind of association with nearly two thousand men, all of them addicts. In addition to my own observations, I rely on input from several fellow leaders including the program's founder and several directors and assistants who have daily contact with everyone. These men have also found freedom from their addictions and have been led by God to care for those seeking the same peace. We discuss and pray about all that goes on in the men's daily lives at length. As I write this, it sounds crazy even to me, and I'm living it!

Now that I've summarized my journey about why I feel I have something valuable to say about this subject, I must give credit where credit is due. I'm sure you've thought by now that living 24/7 in the community for so many years is daunting, or maybe just plain crazy. In one sense you're right. But through all my experiences, the Lord has given me a heart to care for and minister to people who struggle with addiction, as well as their families and loved ones. He has given me all that I need to accomplish what He has asked of me. All the strength, knowledge, wisdom, patience, perseverance, and everything else necessary for the task at hand I've gotten from God through Jesus Christ. He has taught me both through prayer and everyday experiences how to love someone even when they don't want to be loved, or act deserving of anything but correction, or worse. I fall short every day, but I know that He loves me and will forgive me of anything I bring to Him with a humble and repentant heart. I've been able to continue this path only because it is not me alone who is doing it. It is Christ in me. He will give you the same for whatever you do in life, provided you do it in His name.

I hope that by writing about my experiences, what I've learned through years of study, and everyday life in the program that I can help others who are searching for hope and answers. At times my experiences over these past years have been heartrending, but they have also been profoundly rewarding. The pages of this book are the result of those experiences. I hope you find at least some answers to the questions you have. Most of all, I hope and pray that if you have not already done so, you will come to know Jesus Christ as your personal Lord and Savior.

2

THINGS ARE NOT ALWAYS AS THEY SEEM

I can seldom have a discussion with someone about what I do without the question of success rates understandably coming up. This question doesn't have just one answer. Success rates can be manipulated to satisfy practically any desired end. For instance, I was once involved with a trade school that advertised a 96% job placement rate for their students at the completion of their training. This appeared to be true, however when examined a little more closely, most of those placements were as unpaid interns required to perform the internship to complete their school requirements. The school used this as "proof of placement", never following up to find out if any of these students ever obtained a paid job doing what they were trained to do at the school. It's not much different in the recovery field.

What is considered success in recovery? One year sober? Five years, 10 years? And how do you gauge the quality of a life? I've known people who have been sober for more than 25 years who still consider themselves recovering addicts. They go to meetings and recovery-sponsored social events, but still struggle one day at a time to remain sober. That to me is not success, it's only sobriety, and the two are distinctly different. Any facility or program can say whatever they want about success rates, but the truth is that without a clear definition of success, statistics are of little use. That being said, I've seen people become free of addiction, moving on in their lives in full reconciliation with their loved ones. Some have gotten married, started families, started successful businesses, been promoted in their jobs, have attained their GEDs, and some who have graduated college. On the other hand, I've also seen far too much relapse and death. Even one death or one relapse is too many as far as I'm concerned, but unfortunately, there have been more, many more. These failures are not necessary. I firmly believe that, despite what we read and hear from so many so-called "experts," addiction is <u>not</u> an incurable disease.

The Root

One thing is very clear to me, and this is reinforced by nearly every person to whom I counsel or talk; the way to reduce addiction in our society lies not just in the recovery process itself, but in our children. A child's growth and purpose in the family unit must be the primary concern for anyone with children. If young adults have not been taught how to make good decisions in a loving and forgiving household during their early years, they cannot be expected to make good, balanced decisions later in life. The feelings of emotional hurt, rejection, and abandonment, combined with inconsistent or unloving discipline, can push a child to seek love, acceptance, and relief in some very negative ways. Those seeking fulfillment can easily find short-term relief from drugs, alcohol, sex, etc. Unfortunately, these avenues are often not so short term, and can continue until they are in control every moment of the child's life and continue into adulthood.

 The recovery process is something that has only become necessary because of addiction, the roots of which almost always begin in childhood. (I am fully aware of the fact that an addiction can start by taking pain medication for extended periods of time for an injury. I have been closely involved with quite a few people whose addiction began in this way and will address this later in this book.) If we provide a loving home with open communication and set good examples for our children from birth, we will see a considerable decrease in children trying to escape their realities through addiction later in life. I'm not saying that this alone would put an end to addiction, but it would certainly decrease it substantially. The raising of children has far-reaching implications in the parents' lives, from marriage to work and beyond. Broken marriages, multiple marriages, single parenthood, and full-time working parents, if not managed very carefully with the child's best interests in mind, can lead to devastating results. This is not to say that if you have had any of these situations in your life your children are bound to struggle with addiction. My point is that the majority of the people that I have worked with have had at least one or more issues directly related to circumstances during their childhood.

If your children are already grown and on their own you may think that none of this matters anymore, but it does. Knowing and admitting that this may be true in your case will help in figuring out how to proceed in your relationship with a child or loved one struggling with addiction. The first, and arguably most important, thing is to realize that trying to fix or make up for past mistakes is a waste of time and may not end well. Even though you're not the addict, you must accept that you may very well have contributed to the current situation in ways that make sense only to the one struggling. Taking responsibility for past mistakes while moving forward is both wise and healthy. It is essential that there is love and encouragement shown whenever he or she seeks help and is truly committed to changing their life. Talking about past indiscretions, hurts, and disappointments without the presence of a counselor can cause more harm than good. Even when a conversation of this kind seems like it has been productive, the days following may end in relapse. I have seen many cases where a phone call home just to say hello ends in relapse, sometimes days after the call. Even when the call ends on a good note!

It is important to understand that there is no cure all for addiction. Every person's life experiences are different. Even children who have grown up in the same household can have drastically different views of what life was like growing up. Although most of what I talk about in this book is related to mental and emotional issues, there are chemical components to addiction that are significant. It is the chemical component that causes the body and mind to deteriorate. It is also what causes an addict to keep using once they have become dependent on a substance. The sickness that comes shortly after using, known as withdrawal, can be extremely painful while mentally anguishing at the same time. The sickness and anguish will subside if use of the substance is restarted. This is why so many addicts don't make it through the first week of abstinence. For someone that has been using for an extended time, discontinuing use (often referred to as "detoxing") of certain drugs may cause not only pain and anguish, but violent outbursts, threat or desire to harm oneself, and threat of or attempted suicide. It may even cause death by way of organ failure, stroke, or heart attack. Needless to say, no one who has been using for an extended period of time should attempt stopping cold turkey. This is true for alcoholics as well as drug addicts. I know it is common for alcoholics to go on the wagon on their own, but that can be very dangerous. Detoxing from continued alcohol use can be extremely dangerous and can even cause death. There are facilities that specialize in detoxing people from drugs and alcohol. It can take anywhere from three to fourteen days to detox depending on the substance and how long it has been used consistently. I strongly suggest this as the first step in anyone's recovery plan.

3

REALITY VS. FANTASY

At one point in your life, I'm sure that you've watched a baby play with their toys, and almost without exception, a smile comes across your face. Babies go from one activity to the next with either smiles or frowns on their faces, depending on how they interpret the outcome of the activity in their own little worlds. A slightly older child might spend a little more time on an activity, but you can clearly see they are still absorbed in their personal space. In the interaction between the child and his or her toy is a mixture of reality and fantasy.

In the early stage of their lives, children generally remain in the fantasy part of the equation more than the reality part. If you watch long enough however, some part of reality reveals itself to them during this playtime. A toy will break or won't bend in the direction they want it to, or another child wants to play with the same toy at the same time, quickly bringing them into a reality with which they may or may not be pleased. At these inevitable times we can see how that child deals with reality. With proper instruction, guidance, and/or discipline, the child then learns how to begin to deal with reality. Through these experiences, children learn some basic, but very important lessons.

While growing up, a child can have hundreds of "lessons"

every day and the sum of his or her experiences contribute heavily to who that child will become in adulthood. The child will not consciously remember most individual experiences for any significant length of time, but the memories will be logged into his or her sub-conscious mind, collectively adding up to dictate the way that child will react to circumstances well into adulthood, and possibly for the rest of their lives. Considering the number and variety of different environments a child can encounter during their more formative years, we realize there are many diverse factors that eventually result in their view of the world and their place in it. To give you an idea of what I'm talking about I've compiled this short list:

- What type of playtime, if any, does dad have with the child?
- How does dad treat mom and siblings?
- How does mom treat dad and siblings?
- How does dad treat the child's friends?
- How much time does dad spend at home?
- Does mom work or stay home with children?
- How, when, and by whom is discipline carried out?
- How much one-on-one time is devoted to the child by each parent?
- How does the child perceive his or her importance in the family unit?
- What are the behaviors and attitudes of both parents in general?

The home and family environment obviously make up a major part of a child's younger years but additionally there are: other children in school, teachers, the media, other children's parents, etc., all with different views and attitudes toward life, who are being heard and experienced by the child. When the sum total of these messages equal confusion, unpleasantness or unhappiness, the child will begin to rebel or withdraw. The child's personality, which has mostly been affected by their home environment, also plays a major role in his or her behavioral tendencies. Eventually, if there is enough discontent, the child's goal will be to escape the undesired reality they live in, so they mentally escape to a fantasy world that is much more desirable to them.

Then one day the child, roughly middle school or early high school age, (hopefully he or she has gotten that far before moving to this stage), is invited by a friend to have some beer, a joint, a pill, or to participate in some other way to get high, and all of a sudden the unhappy, unfulfilled teen finds that all of the anxiety, fear, etc., are gone as long as they remain in that altered state. That release of pent-up tension is lodged into their subconscious and will now become an option to living the pain of reality whenever it becomes overwhelming. While in this "fantasy land" they can speak their minds, laugh at inappropriate things, not care about what others think of them, and basically forget about all the stress-creating factors that go along with their true reality. If the child's perception of the world is unhealthy, there is little to stop them from going back to that fantasy as often as they can simply because it feels good. However, their constant return to a substance or activity results in becoming dependent, either physically, emotionally, or both. With regards to drug/alcohol addiction, ingesting a substance to enter their now-preferred state slowly begins to become a priority. If not checked, it will become a regular practice, leading to physical (chemical) addiction requiring the addict to use at regular intervals just to keep from getting physically sick. Depending on the substance used, this sickness, known as withdrawal, can be quite painful and even result in death.

At this point, the addict seeks escape, but not necessarily by using a specific substance. If there is nothing else available most addicts will drink alcohol, even if alcohol is not their usual choice. There is usually a preferred substance, but the escape from reality to fantasy is ultimately the desired result. This explains why an addict can be hospitalized or in jail for an extended period without the substance they are addicted to, then return to it immediately after being released. They were certainly substance-free long enough for the physical addiction to be gone, but they're going back to it because the brokenness at the root of their addiction is still there.

Not Just Drugs Or Alcohol

Since it is the escape that is ultimately desired, some turn to diversions other than drugs or alcohol. Food, gambling, work, sex, pornography, video games, internet surfing, social media, watching sports, exercise, and countless other diversions are used. Eventually, the escape becomes so important that the addict will jeopardize everything he or she holds dear to escape the pain felt in his or her perceived reality. Of course, this escape is temporary, and when the fantasy wears off, not only is the unwelcomed reality still there, but so are the consequences that come along with the escape itself. With drugs and/or alcohol, these consequences can be devastating. I'm sure most, if not all of us, have seen or read about these consequences: overdoses and drug-related deaths not just in young people, but in all ages from pre-teens to old age, DUIs, auto accidents ending in tragedy for innocent victims, fights, arguments, domestic violence, murders, neglected children, marital problems often leading to divorce, and the difficult road for single mothers and single fathers, just to name a few.

The desire to escape reality will not leave until reality is no longer painful. And, what makes reality an unbearable pain is not just the pain itself, but also the hopelessness that goes with it. Only God can possibly know when and where all the hurts that contributed to each person's situation happened, and only He can heal them.

The Path Of Destruction

The degree to which addiction has affected our society worldwide is immeasurable. It destroys families, organizations, individuals, and virtually anything it can get a stronghold on. Of course, most people have at least heard of, if not known, people addicted to drugs, alcohol, and gambling, and the devastating effects on their lives. There are also many other "escapes" that can become quite addictive to someone who begins to rely on an act or activity to feel better about themselves or their lives. I know people who are uneasy and irritable in their free time during the off-season of their favorite sport, waiting impatiently for their next "fix" when the pre-season events begin again. Wives feel abandoned by their golfing or bowling husbands, children cannot take their eyes off their mobile phones or electronic tablets, and both children and adults spend countless hours playing violent, mind-numbing video games. Exercise addiction has also gotten to be something more and more people have had to consider in their lives. Caffeine and sugar consumption can also be both addictive and a compulsion.

To address the problem of addiction we must acknowledge the root of the problem. With few exceptions, addiction does not happen with one or two uses of anything. In most cases, the activity or substance created a pleasurable experience that the user yearns for again and again. Think about it for a moment, if there's an area of your life that's not comfortable or enjoyable, wouldn't you try to avoid it or replace it with something enjoyable? Do this repeatedly and you'll find yourself becoming reliant on that activity or substance to help you feel better whenever life doesn't measure up to expectations. When someone is chronically unhappy or unsatisfied in their life, they will do whatever makes them feel better, as often as possible, to escape those unpleasant feelings. Unfortunately, every person that struggles with addiction affects everyone around them in a very negative way. On the other hand, every person who changes their ways and overcomes the struggles and challenges will affect those around them in a very positive way by showing that it's possible to get free from something so destructive.

Yes, there can be freedom from addiction. However, I personally and firmly believe that freedom can only be experienced through a relationship with Jesus Christ. Jesus died on the cross to free us from death and from the strongholds that lead us to death. The scriptures tell us that "*...where the Spirit of the Lord is, there is freedom*" (2 Cor. 3:17). No one has to be an addict for the rest of his or her life. There is freedom for anyone who commits his or her life to love and serve our Lord and Savior Jesus Christ.

Addiction is arguably one of the darkest places one can go in this life, and if there is no one to be the light in the darkness of an addict's life, he or she will be subject to all the torment addiction has to offer. You picked up this book for a reason, so I encourage you to pray and ask the Lord for guidance and trust that He will answer that prayer. My prayer for you is that you find the answers you are looking for not only through this book, but also through prayer and Scripture, and if you have not already, that you come to know the freedom only attainable through Jesus Christ.

4

DENIAL

Denial is a defense mechanism. It helps us avoid painful thoughts and realities about ourselves. When you hear the word denial with respect to addiction, your thoughts likely go to people who you perceive have a problem but refuse to admit it, and you would be right. The tricky part about denial is the way it sneaks in, unnoticed. Many times, people are quick to blame other people or situations for things that are obviously their own responsibility, but they just don't see it. We could all use a reality check in that area. I'm sure you can see a certain level of denial in yourself, while in other areas you are certain that your opinions are completely on-point. I'm not just talking about addicts here. All of us have this tendency and can fall victim to it. You need to question yourself about where your deepest denial lives. For example, if you find that you are running out of money every week before your next paycheck, chances are you have a spending problem. It's not because your income is too low, and your problems would be solved by making more money. The reality is that regardless of your income, and no matter how much money you might eventually make, if you can't control your spending, you will always be short at month's end. Although this example seems very simplistic, the majority of our population is in that exact position.

Most addicts are not born into addiction. There are exceptions, however I'm not talking about them. Addiction is the result of continued unhealthy behaviors and poor decisions while denying those behaviors and decisions are unhealthy and poor. This is the case even with those who become addicted to pain medication while under a doctor's care. It is poor decisions that drive the continued use after the prescriptions run out. I have known and worked with more than a few former addicts who have taken opiates for surgical procedures and extended physical rehab periods, and stopped when the physical rehab ended. They were able to do this because they made it a point to handle the situation and did the work. As an example of what this "work" might look like, let's look at a real situation. I highly recommend this process for anyone who is prescribed opiates for an extended period of time and has come to the end of the prescription period.

Joel had spent years in addiction before entering a recovery program. His addiction had resulted in jail time and alienation from his family. His recovery and healing came through a relationship with Jesus Christ, which he acquired during his time in a Christian residential program. Ten years after his time in the program he needed hip replacement surgery. This would require opiate pain medication from the time of the operation until the end of an extended physical rehab period. The thought of having a hip replaced is intimidating for anyone, but he needed both hips replaced. He decided to have one done at a time, back-to-back. When physical rehab was finished for the first replacement, he went right into the second procedure. He knew being on pain medications for that long would re-ignite his addiction, so he prayed and decided to reserve thirty days in a detox facility following the physical rehab of the second hip. As I am writing this, it has been four years since the surgeries, and he remains free of any desire for substances of any kind.

Why did this plan work? He had been an addict for years earlier in life. Certainly, he would become addicted to the pain medication after taking opiates long enough for two hip replacements and their subsequent physical rehabs. The answer lies in the healing he received when he initially went through a Holy Spirit filled recovery program over ten years prior to the operations. He had been healed of the inner struggles that originally fueled his addiction. He had continued his relationship with God so when the pain medication was necessary, there was nothing spiritually or mentally driving him to desire the escape the opiates provided. He arranged for time in detox to break the chemical addiction his body had developed to the opiates, then walked away from it all. Completely free and without any regret.

One important point in this story is Joel did not deny that the opiates could result in him being addicted once again. Chemically he had become addicted, but he took the steps necessary to remedy that situation because he no longer desired the escape from reality the opiates provided. Had Joel not been free of the brokenness he once had; he would have found multiple reasons why he couldn't stop taking the opiates. In a case such as this it would be easy to blame the drug, the drug makers, the doctors, etc., for Joel's relapse. Ultimately however, it was his faith in God and the healing he had received that enabled him to make the right decisions, avoiding a potentially life destroying relapse.

Denial is a condition that affects most, if not all of us. It's not only the addict's denial that needs to be considered in the big picture of addiction. When parents or caregivers refuse to accept responsibility for their own behavior, their children and eventually society bears that burden. Denial keeps the natural learning and correction process from happening, which can only result in the same mistakes being repeated generation after generation. It will also keep us from repenting of our sins before God. If we cannot admit our missteps, we will never be able to confront and defeat them.

Addiction Cannot Be Legislated

The United States has been fighting a declared "War on Drugs" for over fifty years. The problem existed long before the war was ever declared, but because no one really knows how to fight this war, an astounding increase in the percentage of American alcoholics and drug addicts have emerged. How can that be? Our taxes fund federal drug agencies, state drug enforcement teams, education services, rehabilitation services, you name it. And the results: a marked increase in all areas of addiction. I personally believe the reason these things have failed is that we are missing the point.

Addiction is ultimately spiritual at its core. Families are destroyed by virtually every form of addiction: drugs, alcohol, gambling, pornography, sexual addiction… the list goes on. Addiction deludes a person into believing that there is nothing more important in life than feeding itself. Addiction becomes a seemingly irresistible compulsion, embodying a level of selfishness that's beyond comprehension to those who have never suffered with it. God did not create us to be in bondage to anything in this world, so addiction, by its very nature, defies God's will. As long as we continue to think that it is reasonable and acceptable to expect people to do the right things, even though they've not been taught what the right things are, we will continue to see the numbers climb and the death tolls rise. THIS is extreme denial.

Consider that with all of their perceived intelligence, the scientific community has not come up with a successful immunization against the common cold. Man's intellect is nothing when compared to the knowledge of God. Man's wisdom is nothing when compared to the wisdom of God (see 1 Cor. 1:20). And yet, sadly, there are so many who do not believe or cannot accept these basic truths. Denying God, denying that drug and alcohol addiction are concepts that are formed and authored by dark forces bent on destruction, makes us seek answers in the wrong places. Scientists, doctors, law enforcement, psychologists, psychiatrists, and everyone else who seeks answers in man's intellect will always come up short, because addiction is a truly spiritual issue at its core.

Denial could be keeping you from finding the freedom that's possible through prayer, repentance, forgiveness, trust, and understanding. You may have been affected by an addict in your family, in which case you may feel daunting guilt and shame that seems like it will never go away. This seems unfair, since you're not the one with the addiction. You may search for relief from these feelings by seeking out others who have been through it as well, but if you don't go into the process prayerfully, you may find yourself involved in something that takes you away from God's healing instead of placing you into the arms of Jesus. You may experience temporary relief by changing your attitude, or learning more about the problem, or positive thinking exercises, or meditation, or by any number of other techniques out there, but if that healing is not found through our Lord, it will not lead to true freedom.

Not Just An Addict's Problem

You are not alone if you've dealt with an addict in your life. You have been party to their denial about the severity of their condition, the trouble their actions cause, and on a more basic level, admitting they are addicts in the first place. If you are a parent of or caregiver for someone struggling with an addiction, you may have a haunting feeling that your mistakes are a direct cause of your child's condition. Because this feeling is so painful, you may unwittingly guard yourself from admitting that you may have had something to do with it. Statements of denial, like "he's a big boy" and "he makes his own choices, I have no control over how he acts," or "his sister grew up in the same house and she doesn't have that problem," allows you to place the burden of the blame squarely on him or her. In reality, there

Denial

is plenty of blame to go around, but ultimately, the "blame game" gets you nowhere. This is very difficult to come to terms with, especially if you truly believe you did a good job as a parent or caregiver. The simple truth is that there are no perfect parents. The way children respond to their environment as they grow up presents many challenges, and each child is very different.

As an example, I'll summarize a video I found on the Internet a few years ago. It was a half-hour long testimonial made by Richard, a man whose daughter Marissa had been suffering with heroin addiction. Marissa had been rebellious and strong-willed throughout her teens. By age sixteen she had already begun using drugs and was running with the wrong crowd. Richard's story was of late, worry-filled nights and he feared that she would not make it home. Marissa's eventual all-out addiction led to a stint in rehab followed by relapse. Everyone who knew Marissa was aware of her addiction, but she really didn't care. By age 22, she moved out of her parents' home and had already been through the usual route of multiple possession and prostitution arrests. Regardless of the pleas and offers of help from parents, relatives and friends, Marissa continued down a road of self-destruction. As you can imagine, Richard and his wife Karen were feeling helpless, but they were not hopeless. You see, he was a pastor. Richard and Karen had faith that God would see both Marissa and them through their horrible situation and at some point, in the Lord's time, things would change; his daughter would be healed and go on to live a happy, productive life.

This story then went into a direction that seemed to contradict the good pastor's faith. To get some encouragement and relief from the pain, Richard and Karen searched for a place or an organization where they could attend small group meetings with others experiencing the same kind of pain. They attended meetings sponsored by a well-known organization to support family members struggling with the affliction of a loved one caught up in addiction; however, the mention of Jesus in these meetings was not only discouraged, but many times forbidden.

One would think that a devout Christian would see that forbidding Jesus into the process was an indication they should not be there, but desperation oftentimes clouds judgment. This video was his way of reaching out to other parents of addicts, to share the results of what he learned in these meetings. He hoped that by revealing his story, he would help comfort and encourage others who were hurting in the same way. He stated that after many meetings and personal conversations with other attendees, he had come to the comforting conclusion that Marissa's addiction was a result of her own choices and that he and his wife were not responsible for the poor decisions she made in the past and was continuing to make. He said that although it did not change his daughter's situation, it helped both he and his wife cope with what had become a looming feeling of guilt. By attending those meetings, they had concluded they were not at all to blame. As anyone who has gone through an experience like theirs knows, anything that can bring a lessening of guilt is welcomed. Denying responsibility for anything that turns out unpleasant is certainly one way of feeling better in the moment. But that relief is temporary and will only lead to feelings and issues that will affect virtually all aspects of all involved party's lives in the years to come.

Just by watching this video, there's no way to know what may have contributed to this poor girl's addiction, but a child does not wake up one day and decide to shoot heroin. Obviously, there were factors in her home environment that contributed to her perception of herself and her life. Any attempt by mom and dad to minimize their contribution to the situation is quite definitely denial, which enabled them to conclude, "We didn't do anything wrong." With this belief, Richard and Karen would never realize a need for their own repentance in the whole unfortunate situation. Simply put, denial will never lead to repentance, and repentance is the only road to freedom. When you go before the Lord and accept your brokenness, confess your sins, and have a heartfelt desire to turn from those sins, He will forgive you and cleanse you of all unrighteousness (See 1 John 1:9).

When I've had the opportunity to speak and counsel the parents of addicts, the majority of them do not understand how or why their child got caught up in addiction in the first place. Some think they have it figured out, but their answers are often based in denial of their own responsibility. Excuses like "his father was never around," or "he's always been a rebellious kid," or "his father was a drinker or an addict," or "his mother always gave him whatever he wanted," projects blame onto someone else. At this point one treads dangerously close to enabling their own denial of responsibility.

You are empowered by the will of God to take responsibility for what has happened and to do better for the rest of your life. Conversely, not everything is your fault and you shouldn't automatically search for a way to make everything your fault. This is not about finding ways to feel guilty about yourself because of your actions. You simply need to be willing to accept the responsibility that's yours to accept. If you make it a point to be honest with yourself and check the facts before blaming someone else, you will be surprised at how many times you are too quick to deny or pass judgment.

Developing humility and a willingness to bring your broken self before the Lord with a humble heart and to confess and repent your sins is a cleansing, spiritual experience that will bring about a feeling of closeness with God through Jesus Christ. As the Lord relieves you of guilt, shame, and condemnation, you can then move forward to deal with your situations with a clear mind, not muddied up by your negative self-feelings. This will also help in your willingness to forgive others, because you will have experienced the forgiveness of God in your own life. It is an empty proposition to bury your feelings and think you can overcome them by positive thinking, self-help techniques, or lifestyle changes. These things can, and many times do help for a while, however, the only way to attain deep-down freedom from deep-seated issues is to develop an open relationship with the Lord. The Apostle Paul said it perfectly: *"I now rejoice, not that you were made sorrowful, but that you were made sorrowful to the point of repentance; for you were made sorrowful according to the will of God, so that you might not suffer loss in anything through us. For the sorrow that is according to the will of God produces a repentance without regret, leading to salvation, but the sorrow of the world produces death"* (2 Corinthians 7:9-10; NASB).

I have heard it stated that every addict negatively affects at least twenty people besides himself/herself while in his or her addiction. I believe that to be a very conservative estimate. Because denial is a part of addiction, it logically follows that an addict can be in denial for many years before facing the truth. Unfortunately, that realization comes at a very high cost not only to the addict, but to everyone around him/her. As Christians, it is our responsibility to forgive and love, regardless of the hurt. Some things hurt so deeply you might think it's not possible to get beyond them. Addiction can certainly carve wounds this deep. If you've been hurt so deeply you don't think you'll ever be able to get over it, I hope you will seek godly counsel. Prayerful examination of your situation will bring you to confession and repentance if you pray with a humble heart and seek only the love of Jesus, and the Holy Spirit's guidance.

5

THE ADDICT

There are many different opinions on what makes someone an addict. A telltale sign is that if you have experienced negative consequences due to the use of a substance and have not stopped, you are most likely an addict. Another opinion is that if you try to stop doing or taking something and it causes you discomfort to abstain, then you are probably addicted to that substance or activity. But before I go into the behavior and thought process of the obvious addict, let's take a look at what might be considered by some as borderline addiction.

You will find it much easier to define addiction, or accept someone else's definition, if you don't think you fit into that definition. What I mean is, if you regularly like to smoke some marijuana when you get home from work but have not suffered any negative consequences because of it, you probably would not consider yourself an addict. It is the same for a person that uses alcohol in a similar fashion. The problem with this logic is that unless you stop using long enough for its effects to be out of your system, you won't have any recent, unaltered, baseline behaviors with which to compare your present behavior. In speaking to people about the legalization of marijuana for recreational use, I've found this to be the case. If you are a recreational marijuana user and it hasn't caused direct negative circumstances in your life, you are much more likely to be in favor of legalization. I should mention here that I believe there is very good evidence that medical marijuana use can be helpful when it is prescribed by a medical professional and used as prescribed. However, if you have no need for being in the state that smoking marijuana puts you in, why would you spend your hard-earned money buying and using it? The same question applies to alcohol or any other substance. The most common answers I get to those questions are: "it helps me relax," or "it helps me put the day behind me," or "it's how I choose to spend my off time." All of these seem like perfectly acceptable answers until you consider that if you were at peace with your life, you wouldn't need to use something to help you relax during your personal time. The same goes for anything you find you must do to relax or escape the pressures of everyday life including overeating, working out, playing video games, or any other activity or substance that helps take your mind off of the pressures of life. I've been asked, "Isn't prayer an activity that's used to take your mind off of things?" My answer is no. I've found that when you have a true relationship with Jesus Christ, you come to realize that He is the answer to your problems, not an escape from them. There's a big difference.

Jesus gave His life to free us from the effects of sin in our lives. When you turn away from your sin and ask for forgiveness in the name of Jesus Christ, He offers you freedom from that sin. The next logical question is about belief. Do you believe that to be true? In the third chapter of Hebrews, we are told that *Israel did not enter the Promised Land because of their unbelief* (see Heb. 3:19). Through many miracles, God showed the Israelites that He was with them, and He would provide anything that was necessary to accomplish His will for them to gain entrance into the Promised Land, but they did not believe it. They were afraid of their adversaries even though God had told them He was going to deal with them.

Whenever there is anxiety or fear in someone's life, the root of the problem will not go away by ignoring it, suppressing it, or running from it. They may be able to create distractions or mentally suppress the physical manifestations, but the root cause(s) will remain. There is practically no limit to the ways you can run from internal conflict, but without resolving the root of the conflict it will always be there subtly influencing your behavior and can go unnoticed for many years. For some, the effects of those conflicts can seem trivial. In reality they will eventually lead to discontent with yourself, keeping you from truly enjoying your accomplishments, regardless of how great they may be. For others, it can mean hitting a bottom never believed possible, a bottom that seems so dark and devastating that there is no way to rebound or rebuild.

Jesus deals with the whole person, not just the addiction. He heals us in areas that we don't even realize need healing. An addict can go to rehab after rehab, where they may get their addiction under control, but that doesn't fix the underlying problems or issues that led to the need for escape in the first place. Conflict requires resolution, otherwise we will find ourselves using other methods to escape. Whether we find our relief in drugs, alcohol, sex, pornography, exercise, eating, social media, etc., the internal conflict must be resolved to experience any real peace and enjoyment in life. However, whenever it is found in something that is not greater than us, the escape will be shallow.

A Spiritual Issue

Addiction is a spiritual issue at its core. It can destroy essentially every level of society from the individual to the family, to neighborhoods, to businesses, to government. No one is immune to the effects of someone else's addiction, or to the possibility of their own. Addiction feeds the desires of the flesh, the desires of our carnal nature. In Galatians chapter 5, Paul gives us a list of some of the deeds of the flesh. These include:

- Immorality/Adultery - A strong tendency toward sexual sins.
- Impurity - Fornication - sex outside of marriage.
- Sensuality - Also "uncleanness" or "lasciviousness," all forms of promiscuity.
- Idolatry - Any addict eventually venerates the satisfaction of the addiction above everything else.
- Sorcery - From the Greek word "pharmakeia," where the English word "pharmacy" was derived. In ancient Greek, pharmakeia translates to witchcraft (mind altering substances were commonly used in the worship of evil gods).
- Enmities - Hatred or feelings of ill will toward someone or something.
- Strife - Contention or unrest.
- Jealousy
- Outbursts of anger.
- Disputes
- Dissensions
- Factions - self-seeking groups of people in conflict with others.
- Enviousness
- Drunkenness
- Carousing - aka "rioting."
- And other destructive actions like these.

Most, if not all of these are present in the life of an addict. Early in addiction, an addict will think only of getting high or drunk to relieve the inner pain or physical discomfort they perceive. They become extremely self-driven, meaning that

The Addict

everything in their minds begins to revolve around them and satisfying their own needs to the exclusion of everyone else. They become spiritually open to think and do things they may never have considered had they not succumbed to temptation. An addict can contemplate and execute a plan that seems totally ridiculous to a sober individual. In fact, it would sound just as ridiculous to the addict if they were sober. An addict's compulsion to use, combined with the illogical and morally unbridled thought process that results from regular use, can bring about devastating results.

Generally, by the time an addict decides to get help, they have already left a long trail of destruction behind them. That trail can include family alienation, divorce, loss of jobs, temporary or permanent disability, arrests, jail, or prison time, and even the death of someone other than themselves. All of these are much more common than you might expect. When the addict decides to stop using and tries to turn their lives around, they find it both mentally and emotionally difficult to come to terms with all they have done and who they have become. Unfortunately, many do not stay clean after their first time through rehab. The feelings of guilt, shame, condemnation, despair, hopelessness, etc., become overwhelming and without help and guidance during this time, they will most likely relapse. However, it's not because it's impossible for them to stop using, but because they haven't decided in their hearts that they truly want to change. I've heard it said that relapse is a part of recovery. As far as I'm concerned that's not the case. Relapse is a part of relapse. Period. Relapse is rebellion. It is the selfish mindset that brings on the "I want what I want when I want it" mentality that fuels, then abundantly feeds, relapse.

What To Do

Obviously, there is a chemical component to addiction that can be quite severe. As time goes by, the substance begins to intertwine with the chemical make-up of the mind and body. The need then turns from wanting to get high to trying not to get sick. Although I have mentioned this earlier, it warrants repeating: the sickness that an addict experiences when they don't have their substance of choice can be extremely severe, even resulting in death. This sickness, commonly referred to as withdrawal, can cause a variety of symptoms including hallucinations, vomiting, extreme anxiety, heart palpitations, sudden changes in blood pressure, severe mood swings, depression, mania, and even thoughts of suicide. It is especially important to note that alcohol detox can be very dangerous, and death may occur if the process is not monitored by professionals. It is also very foolish, especially for a long-term alcoholic, to attempt quitting on his or her own.

Unless the drug of choice is marijuana, any daily drug or alcohol user who wants to begin the recovery process should check into a detoxification (detox) center. In my experience, most detox facilities will hold a patient anywhere from 3 to 12 days, depending on the substance, frequency of use, and length of time it was continually used. In the case of marijuana there are not many significant physical withdrawal symptoms so entering a detox facility is not generally necessary. However, marijuana can remain in the system and detectable with a urine test for as long as 45 to 60 days or more, even after only one use.

Even though opiates (heroin, pain meds), cocaine, and methamphetamines take only about 72 hours to become undetectable in a urine test, the physical, emotional, and mental effects are far from gone. For most addicts, a 30-day detox program is adequate time for their physical system to get clean, but not nearly enough time to clean up emotionally or spiritually. During or immediately following the first 30 days, it is extremely important to make arrangements to begin a recovery program. Anyone just coming out of their addiction cannot do it on their own. If you are a loved one reading this, they really need professional guidance together with your prayers and

The Addict

support. Depending on the severity of the addiction, the individual may need to enter a residential program. Regardless of the chosen program or path of recovery, I strongly suggest that it includes God through Jesus Christ. I firmly believe it is the only way to true freedom.

6

A WORLD OF ITS OWN

If you have never had an addiction or been around anyone who has, there are some behaviors and mindsets that may surprise you. First, be prepared for some whining and complaining during their recovery. Remember, this may be the first time in a long time he or she has been drug-free for any length of time, so any little bit of discomfort will seem like the end of the world. You may get a dramatic explanation that sounds like they are experiencing hardships rivaling a concentration camp. You may hear the food is not edible, the staff is cruel and unfair, the rooms are too hot or too cold, the rules are ridiculously strict; you get the idea. They may also ask for money. It's a good bet that if they are asking for money, there's an ulterior motive behind the request. Always check with the staff before giving them anything. Chances are the money is not for what they say it's for and it might just enable them to leave the program. One visiting day, Ralph D. asked his parents for money so he could buy work clothes and boots. They were so excited he was going to be working again after such a long time they didn't think to tell staff about the money they had given him. Unfortunately, it was more than enough for a bus ticket out of town and some "medication" for the trip. So, he left the program and moved in with an old buddy he used to get high with, who now lived in another state.

Manipulation is a survival technique that most addicts learn early on and one at which they become experts. They can become so good in fact, that it's often impossible to tell when they are actually being truthful. Knowing this, it is prudent to set the rules of engagement: that no matter what they privately discuss with you regarding plans, money, or situations, you are completely free to mention the conversation to their counselor or a staff member. This said and agreed, you won't be cast as the bad guy if a situation arises.

In this discussion it is also critical to make it perfectly clear that regardless of whether they are dismissed from the program or if they leave of their own choice, there is absolutely no possibility they can stay with you. The moment you even remotely hint at that possibility, it gives birth to their exit plan. Taking that option off the table right up front might not ensure they stay in the program, but it will give them pause, and possibly take the thought of leaving the program to crash in your home off their future options list.

What Are They Thinking

If you have ever tried to reason with an addict about what he or she is doing to themselves and those around them, you are familiar with the frustration that comes with it. Once a person has become addicted to drugs or alcohol, they become incredibly selfish. Everything in their world revolves around staying in the pain-free zone. I'm not necessarily speaking about their physical pain; I'm referring to the core issues that feed their need to escape reality.

In many cases, a person with a higher level of reasoning will be more skilled in justifying self-destructive behavior. With their own self-talk, they can actually manipulate themselves into condoning their behavior as a viable alternative to whatever is going on in their lives. Intelligence has nothing to do with addiction; it really is about brokenness.

Brokenness can lead an addict (or recovering addict) into a thought process based in fantasy. I have seen countless cocaine and heroin addicts who have been clean for a year or more, but with unresolved core issues, drink "a beer or two with their buddies" only to be back using cocaine or heroin within a few months and sometimes weeks. Why? Don't they remember what it was like to get clean? What sense does that make? I know it sounds incomprehensible to someone that has never been addicted to a horribly addictive substance. For example, a drug addict will convince themselves that because alcohol was not their original drug of choice, it presents no danger of relapse. They're convinced that drinking alcohol cannot be considered relapse since they were never addicted to alcohol. They will go as far as to say they don't even like alcohol. Positive that drinking does not constitute a relapse, they feel free to partake. What they don't realize is that if alcohol was not the problem to begin with, it will not satisfy the driving need for their personal escape. It will, however, awaken their mind and emotions to crave that escape once again. Why a couple of beers and not a couple of iced teas or sodas? It's because there's still an undeniable desire to relieve their internal struggles, like stress, nervousness around people, a poor self-image, anger, guilt, or a host of other issues. Maybe it's a reward for a hard day's work, or a big accomplishment. It's needed because they don't feel any real pleasure in their personal achievements. If you were to consider how many reasons people use to escape their reality, you would find it overwhelming. Listing them all for you would be impossible.

I must also tell you that, in my experience, medical doctors have remarkably little knowledge about addiction. Medical programs give little or no time to addiction, so most physicians might know the chemistry or the science behind it, but they have little knowledge of the affliction itself. I've seen numerous instances where a recovering addict visits a hospital for an injury or illness and informed the doctor that they are in a drug rehabilitation program only to have the doctor prescribe a narcotic. The doctor explains that the prescription is a very low dosage, should only be taken as prescribed, and no refills are allowed. Although the normal safeguards might seem logical to the prescribing physician, the addiction is almost always reawakened. Regardless of the explanation, the warnings, and no-refill prescription, the addict tumbles headlong back into their addiction, obtaining more of the drug by whatever means necessary after the no-fill prescription runs out.

I Only Smoke Weed

Jerry was a bright, ambitious twenty-something who had been smoking marijuana since he was sixteen. As a youth, he and his father smoked it together from time to time and neither of them found it to be out of the ordinary. In fact, Jerry's father reasoned that smoking marijuana was a viable alternative to drinking alcohol because his father was an alcoholic plagued with alcohol-related physical ailments in his senior years. He reasoned he could avoid those issues if he smoked marijuana instead drinking alcohol.

Jerry insisted that he was not an addict because marijuana is not addictive, and he knew he could stop any time he wanted. In his opinion, the only drawback was that it was illegal. But that certainly was no reason to keep from partaking. A few years earlier, when stopped for a traffic violation, the officer detected the distinct smell of weed when the window was rolled down. After a search, the officer found marijuana in his car and arrested him for possession. The judge gave him the choice of entering a rehabilitation program or jail time. He chose rehabilitation. That's when I met him.

On entering the program, he insisted that he was not like "all the other guys in the program" because he only smoked high-grade marijuana, held a good job, had his own place to live, and was not experiencing any withdrawal symptoms. During his time in rehab, he never really submitted to the idea that he might actually have an addiction problem. He stopped using while he was in the program, which only reinforced his belief that he didn't have a problem. He went through all of the motions necessary to fulfill the program's requirements, but when his court-ordered probation period was over, he left without finishing the entire program.

It was more than two years before I heard from Jerry again. This time he called from under a bridge (yes, he told me he was under a bridge), where he had been spending his days to escape the sun. At night he alternated between sleeping under the same bridge, in the woods, and occasionally, homeless shelters. The sad story is, when he left the program, he went back to smoking marijuana, no surprise given his refusal to admit that it may be a hardship for him later in life. However, it was not the marijuana that was the problem anymore.

About a year after leaving the program, Jerry hurt his back. The doctor gave him pain medication to relieve the intense pain, and he liked the way it made him feel. He said it was similar to how he felt when he used marijuana, only more intense. When the prescription ran out and his doctor would not renew it, he went to another doctor and complained of the same "severe" back pain, which resulted in another prescription. He did this several times until he ran out of area doctors, then started buying pills on the street. Eventually he could no longer hold down a job or even pass a drug test to get employment. When he could no longer afford the pills, he found a better, cheaper high with heroin. He began snorting heroin and eventually used needles to inject himself. At this point he was finally willing to admit he had a problem.

Of course, not all marijuana users graduate to using harder drugs. From childhood, Jerry had come to rely on something external to give him relief from his internal struggles. Later in life, he relied on something external to give him relief from his physical pain. If someone needs an external substance or activity to "give them relief" "help them relax" or "forget the problems of the day" on a regular basis, there is a problem that needs to be addressed. If not, the current method of escape may eventually not be enough, and a more potent and damaging escape may be needed. This progression is quite common and not to be taken lightly.

Not For Everyone

Not everyone who uses a substance or medication is going to become addicted to that substance. Some alcoholics use cocaine for an extended period of time during their alcohol addiction, only to stop using cocaine completely. Unfortunately, they continue to drink excessively. Many people "party" all through college, but when it comes time to enter the workforce, they stop partying and get down to business. Many people take pain medication as prescribed, then stop without any problems except the residual pain from their physical condition, for which they will only take over-the-counter pain relievers. Others find they experience withdrawal symptoms when they stop taking a medication. If the withdrawal is too overwhelming, they either enter a facility for a 7- to 10-day detox, or a 30-day program, and that's the end of it. It's a common misconception that everyone who takes pain medication ends up addicted to it. People have various reactions to different medications, and it's no different with pain medications. However, as I mentioned earlier, addiction is not only about the substance; it's about escaping inner brokenness. As in the case with Jerry, problems often arise when someone with an addictive personality coupled with emotional issues is prescribed narcotics. They like the way it makes them feel and begin to abuse the medication instead of following the doctor's orders. Jerry had not used opiates before he hurt his back, but besides pain relief, it brought him that familiar relief from himself only at a deeper and more desirable level. That unfortunate combination of circumstances is not uncommon. In Jerry's case, it led to a progression from what seemed like a harmless pastime of smoking pot to a life destroying addiction to opiates.

I believe that addiction has become more of a problem since drug manufacturers introduced over the counter (OTC) cold and pain medications for children. Sympathetic parents who cannot bear to see their little ones experiencing any pain administer OTC medications at the first sign of discomfort. As funny as it may sound, pain is a gift from God. It is our body's warning sign that something is wrong and needs attention. No one should take medications, especially OTC meds, for every little ache or pain. Children need to develop a reasonable tolerance for pain when they're young or they will be plagued with the distraction of discomforts the rest of their lives. Many people that come through our program request something from the staff for a headache, a toothache, sore muscles, etc., almost daily. Their tolerance for discomfort is minimal to non-existent. As a child, if your parents gave you something to "make you better" every time you complained, it's likely locked into your behavior to do the same as an adult.

Our society has become so relief-oriented that most people don't think twice about popping a pill for every discomfort. It is becoming common to take one pill for each ailment only to have to take another pill to counteract the side effects of the first pill. Additionally, you as a child, and now your children, see and remember much more than most parents realize. When on the phone, if you are talking to a friend and jokingly say that you are so upset over something that you need to take a Xanax, don't think that goes unnoticed. The seemingly harmless comment such as "I need a drink" when things get a little crazy is logged into their little minds for future recall. I can't begin to count the number of people I've counseled who have told me that among their first experiences of using drugs was taking pills they got from the medicine cabinets or handbags of either their parents or a friend's parents. A child has little reason to fear the effects of taking a pill they've seen their parents take, especially if they have a friend urging them on or telling them how great it will make them feel. Add to that the excitement of doing something they are not supposed to do, and you have a perfect storm.

The Nurse's Daughter

Lori came from a good, stable family. Her father was in the airline industry and her mother was a nurse. Because of his job, Lori's father was away much of the time during the greater part of her early years. As she grew older and was able to care for herself after school, her mother began working more hours at the hospital. With quite a few friends and a couple of her friends' fathers trying to fill in as male authorities in her life, Lori became extremely close with several families. Everything seemed to be going well until something happened that looked like a blessing, but it turned out to be quite the opposite.

Just before Lori's freshman year of high school, the family had to move to another state because of her dad's job. It was an incredible opportunity for her father, one that meant a promotion along with a significant income increase. The move, however, did not sit well with Lori. It meant she would have to make all new friends in her first year of high school. It also meant the male leadership that she had come to rely on was no longer going to be accessible. She felt torn between feeling happy for her parents because she saw how excited they were about the new job and the move, and her own fears and discouragement.

It didn't take long for Lori to show signs of depression after the move. They had moved to a small town where the other children had known each other since early childhood. She felt like an outsider and longed to be back with her old friends, but the distance was too great for her to be able to travel back to see them anytime soon. Her mother arranged for her to see a psychiatrist co-worker at the hospital who prescribed depression medication along with visits to a child psychologist. Lori was no stranger to taking medication. Her mother was always quick to give her pain relievers, cold medications, etc. whenever there was something wrong, so she really didn't have a problem with taking medication to help her sadness.

By Lori's sophomore year, the medication seemed to be working or at least it appeared so from her mother's point of view. She was a little more upbeat about going to school and even stayed later most days. Since it no longer seemed necessary, she stopped seeing the psychologist as well. From the outside it looked as though things were going fine, but it wasn't for the reasons her mom thought. Lori had started hanging out with some older boys who were using drugs, pills to be exact. They were taking anything they could rustle up between them. These were not hard-core addicts going into the streets to buy some dope; they were teenagers stealing pills from their parents' medicine cabinets. The change was gradual, and her mother dismissed the little changes as normal teenage behavior. By the end of her sophomore year, Lori had all the friends she could handle, but not the kind her mother would have approved of had she actually met them.

While in her junior year her father became ill and could no longer work, so Lori's mother became her dad's caregiver while continuing to work full time at the hospital. Lori did not show her despair over her father's condition at home because her mom had enough problems. Instead, she started leaning on her new friends for comfort, which came in the form of drugs and alcohol. Pills, of which she preferred Xanax and Vicodin, were plentiful. By the middle of her senior year, Lori dropped out of high school and got a job. When she turned eighteen, she moved in with her boyfriend, and after a short time, she was buying pills on the street using whatever means necessary to afford them.

I wish I could report that Lori saw the error of her ways and turned her life around, but her story doesn't end well. Looking back at the situation, there were many things that contributed to her taking the path she chose. One thing certainly missing from Lori's life was a father, not only her earthly father, but the Heavenly Father. Had she come to know God the Father she would have had something to hold on to other than the older boys, the pills and the alcohol that filled the void when she was most vulnerable. Her compulsion to take pills could have been replaced by faith. You might wonder how I can know this without it actually happening. I've known many people with stories similar to Lori's and in every case, when they came to know and love Jesus Christ, there was a change in their hearts that saved their lives. In cases I've seen where the Lord's love was refused, their lives never seem to get on track. Not all of their stories end as tragically as Lori's. Her life ended at twenty-four years of age in a fatal motorcycle accident while riding with her husband. They were both high. Some find sobriety in a lifelong recovery process where staying sober "one day at a time" is considered victory, and it is. But there is more to life than staying sober. Through Christ we can have freedom, both from our addictions, and from the brokenness that causes so much destruction in our lives.

Do Not Judge

Addiction has affected every level of society: those in law enforcement, judges, lawyers, national leaders, priests, pastors, schoolteachers, laborers, the poorest of the poor and the elitist of the elite. It's easy for someone who has not struggled with an addiction to point a judgmental finger at anyone who has fought or is fighting that struggle. The truth is that we are all sinners, saved only by the grace of God through Jesus Christ. Anyone who does not believe that basic truth is far worse off than any struggling addict who knows he or she needs help but has not yet been able to summon the courage to submit to it. Please try to empathize with all those who are struggling with this affliction and pray that they come to know the freedom that is possible through our Lord Jesus Christ.

If you've never been an addict or had an uncontrollable compulsion to do something repeatedly regardless of the negative consequences, then you will never really be able to understand what goes through an addict's mind. But that doesn't mean you can't be a part of the help they need. In all of the years that I've dealt with addicts I've never experienced a situation where love doesn't strike a nerve. Everyone responds to love when it's from the heart. They may try to deny it or run from it at first, but your loving attempt to help will affect them and stay with them. They will return to it when they're in their darkest hour. Love is not judgmental or accusatory (See 1 Cor. 13). In recovery, we often hear the term "tough love." It's a term used to describe someone treating another person harshly or sternly with the intent of helping them in the long run. Tough love does not have to be mean-spirited. God demonstrated tough love when He repeatedly dealt with the Israelites' rebellion in the Old Testament. Jesus explains His love many times throughout the Gospels with warnings about the consequences of rebellion. When dealing with someone who has hurt you, whether it is through their addiction or anything else, it is only through forgiveness that you can deal with that person in a Godly manner. God is love. When you ask Him to help you love that person regardless of the things they have done, He will answer your prayer. It is ultimately the addict's choice whether he or she will accept any guidance, but the Lord will give you peace about your role in the situation if you approach it with faith, humility, and love.

7

LATE-STAGE ALCOHOLISM

This is not a subject that is discussed much in general, but it's something that I have seen repeatedly throughout my life in many, many people. Because alcohol is legal and socially accepted, having an occasional drink is no big deal for most people. In fact, it seems to be a part of practically every social activity one could imagine. Although drinking alcohol is not a sin, the Bible tells us quite clearly that drunkenness is sinful. Galatians 5:19-21 is just one of many places in scripture that denounces drunkenness. For centuries Christians have debated over whether or not the consumption of any alcohol whatsoever is permissible. However, for our purposes that debate, as well as judgment on the subject, is irrelevant. I believe that drunkenness, not having a drink, is the culprit. If you don't know or insist on denying that you have a problem with controlling your consumption of alcohol, a drink holds control over you. In 1 Cor. 6:12 Paul warns us that although everything is permissible, we are not to be mastered by anything.

Late-stage alcoholism can be very illusive. We consider it normal to have a drink after work, while watching a sporting event, while lying by the pool, while fishing, bowling, golfing, fixing the car, mowing the lawn, before a nice dinner, during a nice dinner, after a nice dinner and on and on, year after year. Most of society includes the consumption of alcohol as a part of almost every aspect of life other than going to church or work. For some, even going to work doesn't hinder drinking. Entertainers, servers, practically anyone in the alcohol service or nightlife industries who has worked with alcohol for any length of time doesn't consider the act of having a drink during work as taboo as other occupations. But generally speaking, a couple of drinks before heading home after a long day of work is really not considered a problem.

But for many, those long days get closer together. Eventually it no longer requires a long hard day, just another day. For some, the weekend is the time they look forward to, anticipating at least one of the two days to really "unwind." Whatever the method of progression, it is still progress; progress toward seeking some substance, in this case alcohol, to do something the body as God created it, is already capable of doing. The concept of needing to ingest something to either help us relax or to enjoy ourselves has become the accepted norm. One does not have to go very far to understand why.

Although advertising has been seen as the culprit in promoting the use of alcohol, the ads have far less effect on our perception as television shows, movies, and now social media. For instance, a lawyer stashes a bottle in his desk drawer but only has a drink after a case is closed, or police officers meet in the bar across from the station for a few drinks to celebrate someone's promotion, or the main character grabs a beer from the fridge and tosses it to his partner when they get to his apartment. You get the idea. As harmless as this seems when life is good, the danger is that life does not always stay calm and easy to handle. When things get a little tense or uneasy for an extended period of time, increased consumption or frequency can sneak up on someone who only has one to unwind at the end of a rough day. When the rough days become more frequent, so does the drinking. It can eventually become a part of the daily routine.

As life continues so does the drinking, and it usually increases because one's tolerance goes up and it takes more alcohol to relax than it did in the beginning. During this gradual increase, it will undoubtedly be the spouse and/or children who notice the subtle changes before the person drinking realizes any difference. If it gets to the point where someone in the family says something about it, they are met with denial and excuses disguised as reasons. Most of us have heard about the denial stage of addiction but hearing about it and experiencing it are two entirely different things. It's usually during this stage of the process that dissension and bad feelings begin to take root. In some cases, this stage can be relatively short and end with the person realizing they have drifted into a bad habit. They quickly decide to quit before it gets out of hand. Unfortunately, this is not always the case, and when it's not, things get more difficult.

As time goes by, the confrontations become more frequent. Gradually, everyday issues and situations become blown out of proportion because of the irrational thinking of the drinking partner. Whenever the issue of drinking is confronted, the stage is set for a major blow-up fueled by denial and frustration. Eventually the non-drinking spouse avoids the issue in an effort to side-step unrest in the home, all the while hoping and praying that somehow things will get better. They seldom do, and the relationship, as well as the family unit itself, is torn apart. The damage is slow but steady and the children feel the downward slide it causes, although they probably won't voice their fears in the beginning.

Initially children do not want to cause more contention between their parents by adding their input, so they tend to act out outside of the home. During this time however, their level of fear and anger increases steadily until they begin to rebel at home as well. By the time an open rebellion begins there has already been a significant amount of damage done to their feeling of security in the family unit. They've seen the divide that has been created between mom and dad and become scared and insecure in their everyday life. Depending on the child, he or she may take sides according to where they feel blame should be placed. The confronter will become angry with the drinker because they have brought this problem into the home. The drinker will become angry with the confronter because they feel that if they were just left alone, everything would be better. Fear, disappointment, and frustration become the norm.

I could continue this scenario with different theories and possibilities of outcomes but I'm sure you get the point. God will provide healing and restoration when we seek His guidance. Addiction of any kind is a symptom of something much deeper that must be dealt with in order to live a healthy life. Simply putting a band-aid on the wounds through behavior modification or positive thinking will not work. As I have mentioned before, addiction is the manifestation of deep problems that have gone unattended. What better way to find answers and relief from the roots of these problems but to counsel with the Designer and Creator?

Tough Times

Bob and Jada were young when they got married, he was 21, and she was only 19. They were very much in love and had their first of four children within a year of their marriage. He grew up in a family that believed in God but did not attend church or feel that faith was a necessary part of life. She grew up in a Christian household attending church almost every week. Bob owned his own business and worked hard in a labor-intensive profession, and Jada worked in the medical field. She had a college education, and he had only finished high school, but this was a non-issue between them. Because of his work ethic and reputation as an honest and fair guy, Bob's business grew, providing a comfortable level of prosperity for his family. There was however, one underlying problem that didn't seem so big when they were young, but eventually grew into an enormous issue.

Bob grew up in a house where his father liked to have a couple of beers every night before he went to bed. This was routine during Bob's entire childhood. It didn't seem to cause any real problems in his parents' marriage that he could see or remember, so when he got married and had his own family he slowly started to fall into the same routine. Jada didn't drink at home, only when they went out to dinner or to a social gathering, and she would generally have no more than one glass of wine.

Since Bob's business was doing well, they both decided it would be best for Jada to be a stay-at-home mom while the children were young. However, as the years passed, business slowed, and things changed for them financially. As times got tougher, the number of beers Bob consumed before going to bed increased. It was very gradual, but eventually turned into a nightly six-pack habit. Then, an occasional stop at a bar after work, sometimes with the guys and sometimes alone, also increased in frequency. Jada didn't want to say anything because she actually felt the same way he did: if he was out busting his butt all day to provide for the family, she shouldn't have a problem with him drinking a few beers from time to time. The drinking however was escalating, and his moods were beginning to change.

Bob became more demanding and controlling. He seemed angry most of the time, especially at night and early morning. Jada couldn't remember the last time they talked without having some sort of disagreement. Whenever she approached the subject of his drinking, he would get angry, deny there was a problem or insist there hadn't been any change in his behavior whatsoever. However, it got to the point where if Bob was not working, he would either be with his friends drinking, or at home in front of the TV drinking. He literally ignored the kids, leaving all of the parenting to Jada because that was "her job." *His* job was to provide the income, although currently there were problems in that department as well. The children kept their distance, mainly because he always seemed angry, but they also did not want to chance being the focus of his anger.

One night Jada tried to discuss the option of going back to work to supplement their income. The children had gotten old enough to take care of themselves after school, and she really wanted to get active in the work force again. Jada didn't expect the reaction she got to that whole idea. Bob blew up, and in his anger, stormed out of the house to calm down. He came back drunk and went to bed without a word.

That was the first time Bob got what Jada would describe as really drunk. She didn't realize that in actuality he had been getting drunk every night for quite some time. His tolerance had increased, which required him to drink more to achieve the same level of escape, but it also made it difficult for Jada to tell how much he had been drinking by watching his behavior or having a conversation with him. You would be surprised how normal some alcoholics can appear when they have actually consumed enough to sink a ship! Bob would normally just drink then go to bed. He never showed the classic signs of being drunk like slurring words, but she knew it was getting serious. They would argue about things they had never argued about before, and whenever she tried to nicely confront the drinking issue, his responses were angry and hurtful.

The arguments increased in frequency and intensity, and Bob continued to deny the problem was either him or his drinking. He insisted that Jada was as much to blame and that she was trying to make life difficult for him. She recommended marriage counseling, which he flatly refused. She also suggested personal counseling, which was met with the same resistance. When asked to go to church with her and the children, he claimed he either had to work, needed to rest from the rough week, or simply refused. All during this time, he continued his pattern of working, drinking, arguing, and stomping out, putting more and more strain on his wife and his children.

Jada held on for as long as she could bear it, until one day she couldn't take it anymore. She confronted Bob when he came home from work late one night, telling him that either he agree to get help, leave, or she was going to pack up herself and the children to move out. He took the option of leaving. He stayed at a hotel for a short time until he found an inexpensive room to rent monthly. As time went on his drinking increased while his family became more and more distant. His business continued to suffer because he lacked both motivation and reliability, until all his customers dried up. Jada found a job and eventually filed for divorce. Bob found himself at the age of fifty, unemployed, divorced, alone and practically homeless. In fact, he was only days away from eviction when he went on a drinking binge that lasted more than a few days. When he finally found his way back home, the locks had been changed. He had hit a bottom he never thought possible. His only options were to go into a shelter or enter a rehabilitation program.

When I met Bob, he had already been at his bottom for a few months. He had accepted Christ as his Lord and Savior and was now looking to rebuild his life with Jesus at its center. I would like to be able to tell you that when he accepted Christ all his problems immediately dissolved while everything miraculously became right, but I cannot. Born-again Christians sometimes try to use this "instant-fix" concept as an evangelical attempt to get people to accept Jesus into their lives. In wanting everyone to experience the saving grace of Jesus Christ, their hearts are in the right place, but this sort of unrealistic expectation only creates disappointment when the person's problems fail to suddenly disappear.

When you accept Christ as your Lord and Savior, your sins are forgiven, your past is washed clean, and you become a new creature in Christ (see Gal. 2:20; 2 Cor. 5:17). This doesn't mean that all of your problems vanish. It means that now, through

Christ, you have the Spirit of God living in you as your source of strength, wisdom, and discernment to live according to His will. However, there's still a battle that continues within you. It's the battle between your fleshly desires and what you now know to be the will of God. It is your obligation to lay your own desires aside to allow the Holy Spirit to work in and through you (see Rom. 8:12-13). Through consultation and prayer, Bob realized that his childhood environment taught him to seek relief from his problems by drinking. His relationship with his father was strained, sometimes contentious, and he couldn't remember his father ever hugging him or telling him that he loved him. The way his father hid his drinking problem from the children was the same way Bob hid from his own children.

Bob didn't grow up with God in the household, so he really had no interest in having a relationship with Jesus until he had lost everything. Without realizing it, Bob's father taught him how to create the very situation he was now living. Since Bob's father did indeed love him and provided for his family, it gave the outside appearance of a normal, functional family. Without the Lord's guidance, we can easily convince ourselves that we are doing things correctly or at least to the best of our ability. Bob and Jada's story is one that plays out for many people every day. If you've found yourself in this kind of situation, please do not feel that you're alone. Bob's struggle is quite similar to literally thousands of people—people who have otherwise lived good lives with the exception of the desire to continually escape reality.

Without a relationship with Jesus Christ, we have no real guidelines. Without God's wisdom we are subject to the influences of our environment. We are vulnerable and easily swayed by societal whims. We are led by our desire to fit in with whatever we view as acceptable at the time, opening ourselves up to be influenced by something or someone else. How do we raise our children? What kind of car do we drive? What kind of house do we live in? What kind of clothes do we wear? Who do we vote for? And the list goes on. Without the Lord, how can you be sure that what you are doing is all you were meant to do with your life?

Be Honest With Yourself

The behaviors that cause the most damage in life are those that come from brokenness. Brokenness causes people to deny problems and justify destructive behaviors as a normal part of adult life. Denial among alcoholics is more common than in most other substances because drinking is both legal and socially acceptable. The problem is further complicated by the fact that there are no formulas to determine how much is too much. The perception of how much alcohol is harmless has been tainted by society as a whole. Drinking has become so much a part of everyday life, our social encounters, special occasions, playtime, and rest time, that our idea of what "too much" really means is usually way off. There are reports suggesting that drinking in moderation is good for your heart or that red wine can raise your good cholesterol, however, having more than one drink negates any possible benefits.

If you honestly look at your motivations to drink and are willing to evaluate your situation, you can begin the path to healing. Below is a list of questions I would like you to consider. I'm not saying you absolutely have a problem if you fit into any of the descriptions that follow. But if you have a tendency or desire to drink more than one drink every time you indulge, it's time to check yourself and your motivations. In fact, if your motivation to drink is anything other than to share a beverage that you enjoy either when it is offered to you or on special occasions, your perception is probably skewed. A good way to gauge this is to purposely make yourself aware of how often you think about drinking.

Consider the following questions:

- Do you think about having a drink when things get a little tense, or when you're having a bad day?
- Do you drink after two or more workdays per week?
- Do you have a thought or desire to have a drink every day?
- Do you drink to fall asleep, or to relax before bedtime?
- Do you look forward to Fridays because you can let go and drink more than other workdays?
- Do you regularly stop to have a few drinks after work before going home, or even at lunch? Do you primarily look forward to social situations because alcohol will be involved?

If you answered yes to some or all these questions, but have not considered alcohol to be a problem, it's time for a reality check. Whether you drink until you are drunk every time is not the issue. It's about how often you think about drinking then act on those thoughts that is significant and can be the sign of a very slippery slope. Step back, take an honest look at yourself, and then ask someone close to you for their honest opinion as well. If you see or hear any questionable behavior, be willing to take action. The first action should be to abstain from alcohol, or any other addictive substance, for a minimum of thirty days. If you have any difficulty whatsoever with this first step, it's time to seek additional help.

8

FAMILIES

I recently purchased a used car. While examining the car's interior I came across the owner's manual, which was placed neatly in the glove box. It was in perfect condition. There were no folds or blemishes on the spine of the binder to show it had ever been opened. I thought back to other cars I had owned and couldn't remember ever reading the owner's manuals. Obviously, this car's previous owner had not either. How did we know what kind of gasoline was recommended or what kind of oil to use? In my case, I recalled something from my childhood days of working in my father's service station. I remembered giving people advice about the general maintenance of their vehicles. All of the information was clearly stated in the owner's manual, yet I can distinctly remember adults asking me, a child, what they should put in their cars to have them run properly. I wonder how many of you reading this know where your car's owner's manual is right now. If you're like most people, you'll only go to the owner's manual when the car stops working. Even then, many of us would rather take it to a garage or ask someone else what to do when it doesn't work properly.

I've heard it said by parents many times, "There is no

owner's manual for raising children." A new bundle of joy lights up your heart, then suddenly you realize the responsibility that comes with it. You quietly contemplate the future, wishing you could refer to a parenting manual. The truth is, God gives us everything we need to raise our children in His Word. The Bible is the owner's manual of life. It explains in great detail how we should live our lives to ensure we will pass through it and into eternal life with Jesus Christ. As Christians, I think we know this is true, but insist upon leaving the Good Book unopened or rarely used unless there is a breakdown. For some reason, it's easier to seek the advice of friends, or fall back on things that have worked in the past than to seek God through His Word for the answers we need. Instead of the Bible being our last resort, it should be the place we start.

In this chapter I've written about subjects that might seem like they're not about you or your situation on first reading. If this is the case, I urge you to prayerfully read it again. Ask the Holy Spirit to reveal what it means to you in your life. As I hope you realized when reading the earlier chapter on denial, it is not a condition that only applies to addicts. If you are uncomfortable or feel a lack of faith, it may be a logical time to stop and pray. Question whether you may have done something in your child-rearing that has contributed to where they are today. Ask the Holy Spirit to help you confront those feelings, confess, and repent of them before the Father in Jesus' name. Confession and repentance are the beginning of healing regardless of how deep the guilt or fear goes. Trust that the Lord hears your cries and is able and willing to comfort you. All true peace comes from the Father through His Son to those who love Him. Jesus said, *"If anyone loves me, he will obey my teaching. My Father will love him, and we will come to him and make our home with him"* (John 14:23). God loves us unconditionally. He knows when we are broken and knows how to minister to our brokenness, which He does through His Holy Spirit. Seek Him with all your heart and receive the peace and comfort of knowing the Lord loves you and is with you.

Widows And Orphans

One of the things the Lord is quite clear about is His desire for those in His Kingdom to look after orphans and widows (see James 1:27; Isa. 1:17). It's not a stretch to realize that spiritual death leaves far more widows and orphans than physical death. A man can marry, then father children numerous times in his lifetime, but can only physically die once. In an addict's life, each one of those marriages may very well end in divorce because of addiction. Suppose that by the time a man dies he was married three times, had two children with each marriage, is survived by two ex-wives and one widow. However, spiritually he has left three widows and six orphans, wives with no husbands and children with no father. Depending on their individual personalities, each child will experience this loss differently in their personal growth. However, one casualty they will all share is that each one of them has been denied a basic developmental need: a present, loving father. If each one of these six children has two children, the next generation will have twelve children being parented by at least one parent who was denied an essential part of their development. The original six children will most likely bring that brokenness into their marital relationships, which could play a part in yet more divorce or separation. The children of addicts have a strong tendency to fall into an addiction in their own lives with the pattern of brokenness passed along to future generations until the pattern itself is deliberately and mindfully broken.

Organizations that offer groups and support for family members of addicts exist, but not many. Most do not incorporate the critical spiritual element; some actually forbid it. The primary organizations, the ones that have the largest membership or followers, don't allow even the mention of Jesus at their meetings. Some make a clear announcement at the beginning of each gathering that attendees must not reference a specific god or belief but may only mention one's "higher power" during testimonies or teachings. Pastors often suggest that family members of addicts attend these meetings to guide them toward some understanding of the issues they're facing. I am sure these well-intentioned pastors are not fully aware of the inner workings of these organizations because they've never attended a meeting. They may not be aware that Jesus is adamantly denied entry into their discussions. The pastor's thoughts and motives behind these suggestions are no doubt well-intentioned, but the result is that the struggling family members are forced to seek strength and understanding outside the protective embrace of God's Kingdom.

When it comes to marriage, I cannot emphasize enough how vulnerable a person is when abandoned by an addictive spouse. Abandonment does not necessarily have to be physical. An addict becomes obsessed with the fulfillment of their addictive desires with little or no consideration for the people around them. Even when the addicted spouse is around, he or she is not really there, and the home environment suffers for anyone living there. It is essential for any Christian in this situation to seek Christian counsel and support groups. Ask your pastor to help you find a Christian counselor with addiction experience.

When hearing a reference to addicts, most people get the mental picture of a junkie sticking a needle in his or her arm, or a drunk slurring words while making a fool of himself or herself. In some cases that picture is accurate, but in many others it's not even close. What about the Internet addict, the workaholic or the sports fanatic? People jokingly refer to a "golf widow" or "football widow" without realizing their spouse's issues can be as much the root of serious problems as a drug addict or alcoholic. I'm speaking of real issues that can cause severe marital problems. And how about the children in these marriages, regularly campaigning for attention from their mother or father, who might be there physically, but are somewhere else mentally and emotionally? In the church, we address these issues lightly through awareness messages aimed at making parents aware of their children's needs. But our society has come to a point where what was once considered a pastime or hobby has become the object of relentless focus. The cause for this near-sightedness is rooted in the brokenness of the family structure, a condition that has become all too common over the past few decades. With each generation we are seeing more of a decline in the family unit. With this decline comes the increase of addictions to not only drugs and alcohol, but pornography, gambling, internet, and social media.

The Breakdown

What happens when a family member's addiction is looming in the background? Although addiction may seem to show up one day out of nowhere, there's actually a long build-up period before one becomes compulsively out of control. A few drugs, such as crack cocaine, can render one addicted after only one use, but in most cases the addictive behavior has developed over a long period of time. All the while, the other family members make concessions and excuses, which enables the addict to justify his or her actions.

Consider a workaholic for instance, whose continual work cycle seems to be necessary to make ends meet. But in so many cases, the ends never meet, and they never will. The addict will continually set conditions in motion that enables their addiction. The thought process can go something like this: the kids "must go" to a private school, we need a faster computer, we need a new car, this house is getting too small, we should start looking for something bigger; you get the idea. On the surface it appears that the person wants bigger, better, or more things for their family, but in essence there's something else involved. Pride, low self-image, inflated sense of self-importance, fear; it all comes down to brokenness. For example, a workaholic doesn't usually get pleasure in the attainment of things, and even when they occasionally do, it doesn't last long. A much deeper issue or group of issues drives them. Having more things gives the appearance that he or she makes more money. Making more money, must mean they are better at what they do than someone who doesn't make as much money. Often, along with the money drive is the desire for power and/or admiration. To further complicate the situation the power addict is typically not really seeking admiration or money. Low self-esteem often drives them to relentlessly seek power and success in an effort to validate their own existence.

Now that we've taken a simplistic view of what might go through a workaholic's mind, let's look at some of the family issues that can result. Even though this may seem obvious, it needs to be addressed. In this scenario, Dad goes to work very early then comes home very late six, sometimes seven days per week. A "pass" is often given for his absence, week after week, which often becomes year after year. If both parents are striving for a better life, mom may also need to be away for shorter periods of time, for which she can also receive a "pass." If both parents consider themselves good Christians, they may try to attend church either Sunday morning or evening, but all too often one of them will have to pass on church because they're out of town, too tired or have some other work-related excuse disguised as a reason. Even though it's becoming more common for both parents to work long hours, it's still usually dad who surrenders Sundays or extra late nights and mom who sacrifices work time for the children. Many families tolerate this situation for the sake of making a better living to have a better life. Over time this situation creates a sense of abandonment in mom or dad as well as the children. Even if mom and dad started off with the best intentions of spending time with each other and the children, their perceived need to have a better life enables them to justify the sacrifices they eventually come to accept.

As you can easily see from the example, trying to deal with all these issues can quickly become overwhelming. Mom, dad, or both become lost in raising the kids while balancing a job or career. Whereas the kids become lost in filling up time that should be preserved for family interaction but doesn't happen because of the parents' work commitments.

Seek The Lord

It's certainly not healthy for anyone to live with a constant feeling of being overwhelmed with everyday life. That's why it is so important to set some time aside each day for prayer. In many cases, I've found that the reason for the struggle to identify God's voice results from not spending enough time in His Presence. The more you pray and meditate on God's Word, the clearer His voice becomes. For instance, you will begin to see that not all things that look like blessings are from the Lord. Negative influences are quite capable of putting promising promotions, extra over-time hours, good deals, and countless other things in your path. If these things are not prayed about, they will look like blessings, when in actuality they are cleverly orchestrated temptations designed to pull you further away from God.

Let's take Bill for example. He has a job he's unhappy with and prayed for God to open a door for new employment. He sent out his résumé, answered ads, and put out feelers to anyone he thought might hear of a job opening in his field. Eventually a company called him looking for someone with his skills and were offering what he considered a generous wage. Of course, he got excited and believed it to be an answer to his prayers. Everything about the job seemed to fit right into what he wanted —even exceeding his salary expectations. The only downside was that it would require him to travel periodically. He would also have to work Sundays occasionally. In his excitement, he chose to believe the job was "obviously from God," and he accepted it without praying or evaluating whether it was truly from the Lord.

As it turned out, the job required more than just a few Sundays, and demanded frequent travel over the weekend. At first, this may not have seemed like a big deal, but Sunday was set aside as Bill's family day with church in the morning, family activities in the afternoon, extra time for personal prayer, and Bible study with his wife in the evening. The extra money may have seemed like a suitable trade-off, but that would just be rationalizing a seemingly good situation turned bad. How could he have known it would turn out like this? Part of Bill thinks he made the wrong choice and the other part reasons that it's worth the extra things he can now provide for his family. They can comfortably pay their bills and have some cash left over for extras. The kids can have better clothes and his wife is pleased that she's not constantly stretching every last penny until it screams. It seemed like it *must* have been God's answer to his prayers. But was it?

Looking at this from God's point of view, anything that takes you further away from Him is not of Him. If you have to sacrifice time with God, you can be pretty certain it's not God giving you the blessing. Add to that the lost family time and you pretty much have your answer as to whether the "blessing" was from God. It is easy to be enticed by better working conditions and more money, especially when you're not happy with your current situation. Considering it a blessing from God makes the decision seem like a no-brainer. However, without prayerfully considering decisions as important as these, you cannot really know if something is a blessing from God, or a false blessing from the devil whose purpose is to pull you away from God. If Bill had prayed about his new job with an open mind to obey whatever God showed him, he most likely would have felt there was something about it that wasn't quite right, even if he didn't know the specific downfalls that were to come.

I've experienced this same type of situation several times in my own life. Having faith, praying consistently, and trusting the Lord to provide the right opportunity at the right time will help to keep you from making this kind of mistake. Through His Spirit, God will reveal what is of Him and what is not of Him. However, this can only help when you pray with the determination to accept and obey whatever you hear from Him, regardless of whether it's what you want to hear or not.

Working Together

Jimmy was an exceptionally bright child with loving parents. He and his sister both attended a Christian grammar school. When they each turned high school age, they switched to public school. His parents had a strong marriage. Dad had a good career and mom didn't work outside of the home until both children were in school. They attended church regularly and were active in their church's activities. Jimmy excelled at almost everything he did. He earned great grades, had plenty of friends that he had grown up with and was very athletic, which became more evident as he approached high school. As a freshman, he made the high school football and baseball teams. Everything was going along well for Jimmy and his family until the month after his sophomore year when his parents announced they were moving and that the move was going to be completed before the next school year started. To say the least, Jimmy was in shock to realize he would no longer attend his home school, but the excitement of the move and the tasks at hand did not give him much time to comprehend what it would all mean.

The family was moving to a state over a thousand miles away. The culture was very different, even the way the people talked was different. One thing that stuck with him over the ten years since they moved, was how the English language could sound so different from one place to another.

In the years following the move, an emotional rollercoaster was set in motion for Jimmy. At first, he and his sister had become reliant on one another. They would discuss how they felt about their new environment, and it comforted them both. In a short time, his sister made some friends at the new school, but Jimmy didn't find it as easy to fit in. His sports ability and good grades threatened the hometown boy's already-proven positions, so the more popular boys ostracized him. There were some schoolyard confrontations, nothing of any real consequence, except that he was feeling more and more frustrated, alone, and angry. To add to his frustration, his sister had become heavily involved with her friends and wasn't around much, so he had to handle his feelings on his own.

Although Jimmy tried to fit in with the jocks, it just didn't work out. He found it much easier to be accepted by another group of boys who weren't into sports or studying but were into having a "good time" instead. It didn't take long before he was introduced to alcohol, marijuana, and a number of other party favorites. Through his junior year of high school he became even more rebellious, angry, and distant to his parents. In an attempt to help him, Jimmy's parents took him to meet with the school psychologist, but by the middle of his senior year, he quit high school.

Within a year after quitting high school, Jimmy was arrested for drug possession and sentenced to probation. The next few years brought more of the same until he was arrested for his first felony—burglary. Finally, his parents felt they had gone through so much pain, anguish, and frustration that they gave him an ultimatum: if he did not get help for his addiction, they didn't want anything more to do with him. This, plus the possibility of five years in prison seemed to get his attention. He pled to the court to sentence him to a drug rehab and was granted his request. His parents were quite happy and supportive, at least in the beginning.

During our talks, it became evident that Jimmy was still extremely angry at his parents for blind-siding he and his sister with the family move, especially with no warning or discussion.

At first, he was not consciously aware of his anger, but the more we talked the more obvious it became. Since his parents had not considered his feelings or desires, he convinced himself that he had little or no relevance in the family. Since his sister found some friends early on and he didn't, he perceived that as another deficiency on his part. His self-image had been damaged and he felt nobody cared about how he felt and there was no one he could rely on. Now, because of all the trouble he had caused himself and everyone else, he was convinced that everything was beyond repair.

With a lot of prayer and hard work, Jimmy turned his life around. The judge withheld adjudication on the burglary charge, and he easily completed his mandatory community service as well as the recovery program. His job appeared to be leading to a career, and most importantly, the relationship with his parents was restored. All this within one year. Had there been communication within the family throughout the process of relocating, things would probably have turned out much differently for Jimmy. He could have been made to feel that his feelings about the move were important to his parents. This would have made it much easier for him to express those feelings to them when he needed to the most.

A lack of communication in the family unit makes children feel their role in the family is insignificant. This is especially evident in pre-teen and teenaged children. This is not to say that you should lead your children to think they have more say in matters than what their maturity allows. However, not making your children a part of the discussions about things that will directly impact them can yield unpleasant consequences. Communication is key in the parent/child relationship. Children need to have confidence in their position in the family unit. Parents many times fail to realize the importance of keeping their children in the loop. You may think they're too young or immature to understand, but without open and honest communication, you can't possibly know where they stand. Take the time to explain and lovingly address their thoughts, fears and concerns. Children can carry emotional wounds with them throughout their entire adult lives regarding things that may seem to be of little significance to a parent at the time. Often, these wounds come from perceptions that could have been avoided had there been a clear, trusting line of communication.

The communication I just explained will become an accepted part of your family life if you come together regularly to worship God. Worship is not just singing and dancing. Worship is anything that gives God glory. You can worship as a family by praying at mealtime, setting aside family time each night to talk about each other's day, and reading Scripture. Maybe attend church gatherings in addition to Sunday church. Try a small group Bible study or a church sponsored community outreach project. Children need healthy activities with other children of their age group. As they get older, there are plenty of Christian activities in which they can participate, such as skateboarding events, golfing, bowling, baseball, football, even Christian skydiving and mountain climbing. These activities will help build a strong foundation while keeping them focused on what really matters in life. The rewards will be life-long, and the love of God through Jesus Christ will be passed on by your children to the next generation. That's what is meant by the term "worshiping God!"

A Note To Fathers

Jimmy's story is by no means unique. I've seen the same kind of issues again and again. A considerable percentage of people who suffer with addiction, both men and women, have some sort of brokenness in their relationship with their father. The father is the spiritual head of the family. Figuratively, it seems that the dark forces have seriously acted on the premise that if you want to kill the body, you just need to cut off the head.

A society cannot flourish without good leadership. Leadership begins with an understanding of what a leader is, and what a leader is not. Jesus showed us through His own life what it means to be a true leader. Through His life we see that a godly leader is a servant who is willing to lay down his life for his flock. He will always put them first, before his own desires. A Christian father's primary responsibility is to lead his family in prayer and in worship. He can only do this effectively if he puts God first in his own life.

For any father reading this, I would like to offer some important advice. Love your children by showing them that you love God first, then tell them that you love them and care for them. Hug them, root for them, give them encouragement when they are down, and communicate with them on their level with as much love as you can possibly muster. Show them that you care even at times when you need to discipline them. A loving father disciplines his children out of love, not out of frustration or anger. Let your yes be yes and your no be no. As an example to them, live your own life as true to God's word as possible and do not compromise what you know to be right before God for the sake of making them happy or satisfying their fleeting whims. Your children are God's children, and they are His gift to you. The Lord entrusted them to you to teach them His ways and to look after them as they grow into adults who will look to Him for their every need. When you look at your children in this light, you will undoubtedly see areas where you have fallen short. Repent and ask for the Lord's forgiveness and for the strength and wisdom to do better, knowing in faith that He will answer your prayers.

Even though you do your best there is the possibility that one or more of your children may go in the wrong direction and turn away from the things you tried so hard to teach them. In these instances, the best thing you can do is pray and trust in God's protection. If they had a good foundation in the Lord early in life, it's very likely they will return to Him after their rebellious years have passed. Even if they didn't have that foundation, once you go to God in repentance and pray for their well-being, trust the Lord will answer those prayers. Keep praying, keep forgiving, stay involved, and never lose faith that the Lord hears and answers your prayers. He might not always answer them in the way you want them answered, but always for the good of those who love Him (see Rom. 8:28).

9

CHOOSING A RECOVERY PATH

Before doing or planning anything, it's important to determine if legitimate mental health issues exist, or if drug or alcohol use is causing manageable mental health issues to appear more serious than they really are. If you are unsure in any way, you should seek professional medical advice before choosing a recovery plan.

The behavior of an addict can closely resemble that of someone suffering with a variety of mental health issues. Depression, rage, disassociation, hallucinations, severe mood swings, and suicide are just some of the behaviors and manifestations an addict can display that may or may not be mental health issues. Arguably, addiction itself can be considered a mental health issue. However, there's a big difference between addiction as it pertains to behavior and spiritual brokenness, and addiction as a result of a chemical imbalance or a more serious mental illness.

If you suspect mental health issues and decide to consult a physician, it's important to choose a doctor who has substance abuse training or treatment experience. In my experience, when a physician who doesn't understand addiction treats an addict, they prescribe several medications to cover all bases. In our program, it is not uncommon to have people arrive with as many as six different medications, most of which they had not taken prior to entering a hospital or detox facility. Most commonly, they are medications to treat bipolar disorder, depression, anxiety, sleeplessness, heart-related issues, stomach distress, and ADHD. In many cases, all of these medications are prescribed for this one person after only 5 days in a detox facility or hospital. This methodology is drug overkill, since it's completely unknown at this point how that individual will tolerate or respond to each drug's side effects or all of the drugs' interactions. However, hospitals often use this approach to stabilize detox patients just long enough to release them from the hospital. Flooding a person with new medications while the body is changing due to sobriety may hinder rather than help in the long term. Unless they get immediate help with their addiction, it is very likely they will return to using their drug of choice when the prescriptions run out, if not before.

All of this can be confusing to a sober person, much less someone who's not thinking clearly. If you're the person helping another with this process, do it with love and understanding, however don't give in to their requests if you don't feel right about it. Your gut instincts are critical at this time since the person you're helping will not be able to see things clearly, understand his or her feelings, or navigate the challenges in the best way.

Fear and uncertainty can prevent an addict from following through with a recovery plan right from the beginning. Do not give them any money or support that enables them to put off entering a program. Very likely, you may have to give them a choice: to get help or you will have to wash your hands of the situation. This may be extremely difficult to do, but it will not help the addict to give in to their demands. It may be a struggle, so pray, ask the Lord to guide you, and trust that He will provide the way.

Short-Term & Outpatient Treatment

In most cases an addict will not realize they are an addict until there's some form of negative consequence in his or her life directly related to their use of drugs or alcohol. Generally, if someone needs to experience negative consequences before they realize they're addicted to something, they most likely have issues that need to be addressed beyond the drugs or alcohol themselves. To illustrate, let's look at a common situation I saw play out a few years ago.

Beth, a healthy twenty-four-year-old, was involved in a car accident. As a result of her injuries, she was in tremendous pain on a continual basis. The doctor prescribed an opiate-based pain medication. It took quite a while for her injuries to heal, during which time she took her medication as prescribed except for a few times when the pain seemed worse than usual. She quickly realized that when she took more than was prescribed, she didn't like how she felt. When she described the feeling to me, it was much like an addict describes how they feel when getting high. She was euphoric and had a burst of energy, only to fall into a depressed state, but with a desire to take more medication to relieve the depressed feeling. Because she didn't like this feeling, Beth decided to stick with the prescribed dosage from then on, regardless of the pain. When her prescription ran out, she started feeling withdrawal symptoms. She contacted the doctor who suggested she consider a short detox program. She took his advice, went to detox, and never wanted any part of that drug, or any other drug again.

Beth was not an addict in the sense that I'm addressing in most of this book. Yes, she had briefly become addicted to pain medication, but the difference was she didn't like how it made her feel. This indicated that she was comfortable with her reality or was at least comfortable enough not to feel the need to escape. The euphoria was unwelcomed and unnecessary, and she would actually rather experience more physical pain than have the feeling of being high. Her addiction was purely chemical. Consequently, when her physical addiction was gone the entire issue was finished. However, many people want to keep returning to that euphoric feeling once they have experienced it. That is when the problems begin.

Short-Term Solutions

Outpatient programs, as well as short-term residential programs such as the common 30- or 90-day programs, may or may not be enough recovery time, but one of these programs may be an option as a first-time recovery attempt. There are some pretty good indicators to help determine if a short-term program will be effective. The addict must answer these questions honestly before deciding if a 30- or 90- day program is a viable option.

1. What is the longest time you've gone without using any drugs or alcohol in the past year?
2. How many different types of drugs have you used more than a few times?
3. Do you feel sick or anxious when you're not using?
4. Do you think about using when you're not using?
5. If you've gone more than 7 days without using and then started again, what made you want to start?
6. How many negative consequences have you experienced that are drug- or alcohol-related?

If they have not had any time without using, use more than one drug or mix drugs with alcohol, think about using when they're not, and get sick every time they stop, a 30 or 90-day program will not be the best route. Additionally, if there's a pattern of negative consequences, there is likely to be a serious problem that cannot be remedied by a short-term fix. Many people begin their recovery path in an outpatient or 30-day program. This is sometimes dictated by their insurance coverage limits. It may also be because they don't realize the depth of their problem, or they don't want to disrupt their lives for any more time than absolutely necessary. In these instances, the 30 or 90 days invested may be wasted. It really makes no sense to waste time and money on an outpatient program if there's no accountability system set up within their everyday lives. It is much too easy to have a few beers (or more) between sessions without anyone noticing. If the primary motivation for entering a 30- or 90-day program is to "get back to work as soon as possible" it could very well be a fatal mistake.

For these reasons, I feel it is essential to seek the help of someone experienced in addiction recovery. If possible, a knowledgeable counselor or intake specialist you feel you can trust will be honest with you, and not just want to sign you up to their program. It would be beneficial to get several opinions from both long-term residential and short-term counselors. I suggest you do not take the advice of anyone who entered but did not complete a program. Also, talking to someone who attends AA meetings, 12-Step meetings, or overcomer groups might seem like a good place to start, but that's not always the case. They may know recovery as it pertains to them, but probably will not have the experience necessary to give sound advice for your situation.

Finally, and most importantly, there's nothing more powerful than prayer. Seek the Lord with an open and willing heart. Ask Him for guidance and He will open the doors you need to get the answers you seek. Whether you are someone trying to help an addict, or you are the addict, God will answer your prayers. If you're struggling with an addiction, don't think God ignores your prayers because of the things you've done. He will come to you where you are and guide you in the way everlasting (see Psalm 139:23-24).

New Beginnings

You can pursue several different avenues when considering a recovery program. Since I believe that most addiction is spiritual at its core, you would be right to assume that my perspective of recovery is in line with my beliefs. However, I have not come to this belief without direct experience with the most common alternatives. In addition to working with countless men who have been through practically every type of recovery program available, I have experienced some of them myself.

I'm certainly not suggesting that any given recovery program or type of program is completely ineffective. On the contrary, they all have their good points and can certainly help in one's battle to find relief. When searching for a program, many people ask the question, "What is the program's success rate?" This may seem like a logical question; however, it is nearly impossible to answer. One reason for this lies in the definition of success. If you base your evaluation on simply making it through a program, you will get a very different answer than if you were to gauge success by how many people stayed clean for a year or more after completing the program.

A second consideration is the quality of one's life after the program. I've known many alcoholics and addicts who have been clean for years but are miserable in their everyday lives. Of course, they'll admit their life is better sober than it was when they were using, but they're still struggling. To them, every day they don't drink or use drugs is a victory, and in some sense it is. However, if ten, twenty, even twenty-five years later they are still going to addiction recovery meetings, talking about the struggles of not using and battling the same things they were battling a decade or two ago, there is something wrong. This sad scenario illustrates someone who has only learned how to stay sober, usually by being around other people who are fighting the same battle. It seems they've only learned how to find comfort in meeting with a group of others to lament about their life and listen to others do the same.

In your search for help, you will run across many very different types of recovery programs and I recommend you keep an open mind, research thoroughly and not dismiss an option based on generalities. The three most common types of recovery programs are: 1) non-faith-based *secular programs*, 2) *faith-based programs*, and 3) *Christian programs* that put God through Jesus Christ at the center of the process. My obvious bias is the Christian program, since it incorporates dealing with the underlying issues rooted in the soul along with freedom from the physical and social hardships of addiction. In the sections that follow I give an overview of these three types of programs. Every program reflects the attitude and heart of its leader(s), so be thorough in your investigation.

Secular Recovery Programs

Secular programs rely mainly on scientific and medicinal-based theories and remedies. A secular program might include behavior modification, life skills training, psychiatric and psychological evaluation and its resulting treatment, as well as medication therapy. A new term that has surfaced lately is evidence-based medication therapy. This simply means taking drugs to stop taking drugs. It is based on data revealed through controlled studies. The medications that I've seen prescribed in these evidence-based medication therapy programs are sometimes as addictive as the substance the addict wants to quit using. At least some, if not all of the prescribed anti-drug medications will cause as much or more pain and sickness during the detox process than the user's original drug of choice. Another downside of this approach is that use of the anti-drug commonly leads to a new addiction. Many men who have come through our program have struggled through these types of recovery processes, only to require another program to detox from the anti-drug.

Since addicts typically do not handle pain or discomfort well, the "take something to help ease the pain" recovery method can sound quite attractive, but there are potentially negative consequences to consider for this avenue. While a secular recovery program is not necessarily completely void of spiritual or faith aspects, the primary focus will be from the scientific or medical point of view.

Faith-Based Recovery Programs

In general, faith-based recovery programs integrate the spiritual aspects of recovery with medical therapies. The word "faith" in "faith-based recovery program" is translated as "worshiping your god" but it does not carry any qualification as to what god you worship or even that your god is a higher power. In these programs, everyone addresses the "god that they worship" on the spiritual side along with behavior modification, life skills training, evaluation, medical/medication therapies, lifestyle training and meditations or prayers. A faith-based program will have a spiritual component allowing the client to determine who and/or what and how they will worship. The dividing line between a faith-based program and a Christian program is that Christians worship the one Almighty, True God, which is only possible to do through belief in His Son Jesus Christ (see John 3:16, 14:6; Romans 10:9). A non-Christian faith-based program is worth consideration if you believe in anyone or anything other than Jesus Christ, however, if you are a Christian, I do not believe this will be a robust or sustainable alternative.

Combination Recovery Programs

Some programs combine the faith-based and medical avenues of recovery. They often place equal importance on both the medical and the spiritual aspects of recovery. If moderate to serious mental health issues are involved, this may be an option to consider first. In a combined program at a medical facility, the mental health issues are addressed, usually involving medication to chemically balance the mind and body. This avenue of recovery is individual in nature, meaning a physician will diagnose the extent of the patient's mental and physical needs and recommend a treatment plan unique to that individual. While the chemical imbalance issues are being treated, there will usually be meetings and counseling that address behavioral issues. These will usually involve multiple participants in both small groups and larger meetings as well as one-on-one counseling.

The cost of this type of facility can be staggering. Insurance may cover some of those costs, but only for a short time. Unfortunately, it is common for the doctor to suggest a treatment plan that is in line with the length of the insurance coverage, which is usually thirty days. Someone who has an addiction problem serious enough to require residential treatment generally needs much more than thirty days of residential treatment. Relapse after a thirty-day program is very common.

If this type of facility is necessary because of the medical needs of the addict, I suggest there be a plan to continue treatment in a non-medical recovery program immediately following the completion of the medical program. The cost will be much lower without the constant medical supervision, but the recovery process can continue in a safe environment.

Twelve Steps

Alcoholics Anonymous (AA) is a 12-Step Program that began as a Christian organization for alcoholics. The steps themselves were formulated through Biblical precepts. Narcotics Anonymous (NA) is an AA program for drug addicts. Although it's focus is on recovering drug addicts, it is virtually identical to

AA. Its founders were Christian men who believed there was hope for alcoholics through the saving grace of Jesus Christ. In an attempt to reach out and accommodate more and more people, the reference to God was changed to "a Higher Power," or "God as you understand him." This was, in effect, an open door for the devil to separate the 12-Step Programs from God through Jesus Christ. This alone condones worshiping "gods" other than the One and only true God, in other words, idol worship. Many 12-step meetings have become void of belief in the power of Jesus Christ. Jesus was quite clear in His statement, *"I am the way, and the truth, and the life. No one comes to the Father except through me"* (John 14:6). It does not get much clearer than that! It would cause quite a stir in most 12-step meetings if one were to stand up and state with total conviction that "there is only one God, and only one pathway to God, which is through belief in His Son Jesus Christ. Through Him we can receive total freedom from our afflictions." Yet, in an effort to reach more people, a few of the original members were willing to sacrifice quality for quantity by allowing the Gospel to be watered down. This meant less talk about Jesus and more talk about themselves. Without Jesus, the steps become a process to stay sober one day at a time. With Jesus, there is a road to freedom.

Looking at this from the point of view of someone that does not believe Jesus is the Son of God, the question arises of why should they be made to feel uncomfortable in an organization that's supposed to help them stop drinking or using drugs? For the unbeliever this point is valid, and I believe 12-step organizations should be available for everyone, regardless of their religious beliefs. However, without the power of the Holy Spirit, abstinence becomes a lifelong battle. In addition, without the freedom that comes through a relationship with Christ, recovery becomes a stronghold, always vying for attention. As a brief example of what can happen when we look to our own devices for comfort, one's experience through a 12-step process might look like this:

Let's say you have been attending 12-Step meetings for some time and feel as though you've done well in your recovery, at least you are sober. You wake up in the middle of the night and for some reason you are really struggling with staying sober. You call your sponsor, but he doesn't answer his phone. You leave a message that you are afraid you're going to use and really need to talk. The desire keeps growing. You grab your Big Book (The Official Book of AA) and read a couple of encouraging stories but the urge continues to grow. There are no meetings at this time of night, so you turn to your higher power, which in this story, is a motorcycle. Yes, I've met many an alcoholic and drug addict whose higher power is a motor vehicle, especially motorcycles. You get on your higher power for a ride—that usually works. You take off and because you are lost in thought, your speed creeps up. The next thing you know blue lights come up behind you. You get cited for speeding by an officer who is not swayed by the explanation of your personal struggle. Now you find yourself wanting to use even more than before all of this started. Back on the cycle and heading home, lights from the 24-hour grocery catch your eye. Deflated, lonely, depressed, and angry you buy a single can of beer "just to take the edge off".

After all the time, care, and effort you've put into recovery, one unanswered phone call and one fast ride wiped it all out in a single night. Attempts at working the steps while eliminating the Biblical guidance necessary to fully understand them will bring results that fall far short. The real power of the steps is through Jesus Christ, not the steps themselves. The foundation of the 12-steps was scriptural. A quick browser search of the Christian 12-steps will yield lists of those scriptures. Taking Jesus out of the process of working the steps is like breathing in a room with no oxygen. You can go through the motions, but it will not produce the desired effect. Freedom from bondage comes through belief in Jesus Christ, not by performing a list of tasks.

Christian Recovery Programs

In Christian recovery, God through Jesus Christ is at the center of everything. It's not about the addict, the brain, the chemicals, the emotions, or anything else that might detract from the sovereignty of God. Addiction is an incredibly selfish existence, which in every aspect opposes God. To an addict, finding relief from the pain or discomfort of being who he believes he is becomes the most important thing in his life. Eventually addicts will continue to use their escape of choice regardless of how it affects not only them, but everyone else around them. Their world shrinks down to acquiring whatever he or she needs to bring relief. They will do anything necessary to escape the sickness that comes from not using, or to escape the pain that originally caused the addiction, or both.

To demonstrate how an addict perceives life, I often use a basketball analogy. If you hold a basketball in front of your face until it touches your nose, the only thing you will see is the basketball. It keeps you from seeing anything else, no matter how close the other things are. However, when you lower the basketball into dribbling position you can see everything around you and the basketball no longer consumes your vision. It's the same with addiction. It seems so big that you can't see anything else in your life but the addiction. Either continuing in the addiction or beginning recovery can be the basketball touching your nose. In secular as well as some faith-based recovery methods, the basketball of recovery is just a replacement for the basketball of addiction. Either way, how the addict views life and the world they live in can be terribly short-sighted.

Christian recovery puts God through Jesus Christ above all things. In the first two chapters of Genesis, we see that God not only created all things, but gave special attention to man. He saw that man needed a helper, a companion, so he created woman. He gave the man authority to name all the animals. We are His special creation. The Apostle John explained Jesus Christ to us in his Gospel: *"In the beginning was the Word, and the Word was with God, and the Word was God. He was with God in the beginning"* (John 1:1-2). And John continued: *"The Word became flesh and made His dwelling among us. We have seen His glory, the glory of the One and Only Son, who came from the Father, full of grace and truth"* (John 1:14). We are told how God demonstrated His unconditional love for us: *"For God so loved the world that He gave His one and only Son, that whoever believes in Him shall not perish but have eternal life"* (John 3:16). John goes on to quote Jesus telling us something that is incredibly encouraging, especially in troubled times: *"For God did not send His Son into the world to condemn the world, but to save the world through Him. Whoever believes in Him is not condemned, but whoever does not believe stands condemned already because he has not believed in the name of God's one and only Son"* (John 3:17-18). Then John later quotes Jesus as saying: *"I am the way and the truth and the life. No one comes to the Father except through me"* (John 14:6).

When a person enters Christian recovery, they find they are not alone. Not just because there are others in recovery with them, but because we are all unconditionally loved by the One and Only God through His Son Jesus Christ, regardless of what we have done in the past. We are not condemned because of our past but forgiven through our belief that Jesus gave His life for us. We are not defined by our sinful past, but by the love of God through Jesus Christ. He wants to heal us of anything that causes sin in our lives and to free us from our bondages. Christian recovery is about the whole person, body, soul, and spirit. Jesus told us *"So if the Son sets you free, you will be free indeed"* (John 8:36).

Recovery needs only to be a season in the life of addicts, followed by a season of healing and growth as they see who God really made them to be. Then, in God's time, when that season has passed, the addiction will no longer appear like the basketball it once was. It will become part of what God uses to increase their wisdom. Through the renewing of their mind, they will become a blessing to others, giving glory for all things to God through Jesus Christ.

Counseling

To many, counseling is considered a sign of weakness. Those who embrace that view believe one should be able to deal with their own problems and shouldn't need to tell someone else, especially a stranger, their deepest, darkest thoughts, and feelings. People feel this way for many reasons. One is fear—fear that revealing what they know as the ugliness inside themselves would only add to their current problems. Next is pride. Admitting there's something inside they can't figure out and fix by themselves doesn't align with their inflated self-image. And then there's hear-say. Listening to someone who tried counseling and speaks about it negatively makes it easier to dismiss, especially if some fear or pride is already in play. In his second letter to the Corinthians Paul writes: *"That is why, for Christ's sake, I delight in weaknesses, in insults, in hardships, in persecutions, in difficulties. For when I am weak, then I am strong"* (2 Cor. 12:10). God will work through others to guide us when we can't find our way, but we must come to Him with a willingness to submit to His guidance. That guidance often comes in the form of a counselor.

Counseling in and of itself does not fix anything. It's not like getting a shot of antibiotics for an illness. The results produced through counseling are in direct proportion to the amount of honesty and work you are willing to invest. If you aren't honest with a counselor, your sessions will not be fruitful. Some people respond well to counseling, giving themselves entirely to the process, while others will not. For some, counseling sounds like an easier answer than a residential program. For this reason, I don't think the person who needs help should be the person to determine whether counseling alone is an appropriate avenue for their recovery. If the choice is between entering a residential program and outpatient counseling, most will choose the counseling route because it seems like less of an inconvenience. It makes no sense to invest time and money into outpatient counseling if the decision to do so is based solely on keeping your job, not being away from your family or some other inconvenience. The path of least resistance may very well lead to relapse, especially if there is little or no accountability involved. If you've been sober for an extended period of time more than once and relapsed, chances are you should seek residential treatment. I recommend you seek an addictions counselor for an evaluation or talk with someone you know who has been there and is fully familiar with the recovery process. Convenience should be of little consideration when determining your recovery strategy.

Accountability in the recovery process is as important as counseling. When addicts use, they usually lie about it. They lie to their loved ones, to the counselor, and to anyone else who questions their behavior. If you're dealing with an addict, do not assume that you'll be able to tell when he or she is using. There are many, many addicts that can use and not show any obvious outward signs. The only way to tell for sure is through a urine or blood test. Unfortunately, even with a urine test it's still hard to be sure. Products are sold over the counter that can turn a urine test to a false negative. If you are trying to help someone who really doesn't want to change, they'll be able to fool you if they're committed to doing so.

In reality, if someone has been struggling with an addiction, then experienced sobriety only to relapse again and again, counseling alone will not be enough. It's time for residential treatment. Another sign of a need for residential care is a history of drug or alcohol use that leads to encounters with law enforcement or improper behavior toward other people or themselves. If abuse of any kind is a part of the addiction, immediate treatment should be sought. Abusive behavior will not change until the addiction is dealt with in a serious manner. As part of that treatment, there will most likely be one-on-one counseling and group counseling in an environment that will obtain the best possible outcome.

The thought of entering a recovery program, especially a residential one, can be a frightening experience and should not be considered lightly. Conversely, it should not be used as an alternative to some worse-sounding consequence such as jail or homelessness. The main ingredient is the person's willingness to do whatever is necessary to win the battle. Everyone has a choice and a chance. Some battles require more fight than others. Have faith, put one foot in front of the other and do not accept defeat. There is always hope in Jesus Christ.

The Stronghold Of Recovery

Recovery often becomes a stronghold for those who dedicate their lives to it. Allow me to explain what I mean by this. Recovery most often starts with a belief that once a person is an addict, he or she will be an addict for the rest of his or her life. This is not true, but if someone believes it, it becomes truth to them. Armed with this preconception, they enter recovery being told the only way to ensure a life of sobriety is to never lose sight of the fact that they are addicts, and to make recovery a part of their lives. This makes attending meetings and staying connected to a sponsor appear to be the only avenue to long-term sobriety. The recovering addict then learns that as long as he or she is faithful to the process of attending meetings and staying connected to other recovering addicts, he or she might have a good chance of lifetime sobriety. If they stop attending meetings, they will eventually become weak and relapse.

God did not intend for any of His children to live a life held back by bondage of any kind. Instead of the path to freedom, recovery has become a permanent holding place for those who seek help with their addictions. Paul clearly told us: *"Now the Lord is the Spirit, and where the Spirit of the Lord is, there is freedom"* (2Cor.3:17). The "freedom" Paul refers to is freedom from all bondage. Many people in Paul's era were quite familiar with bondage, or slavery to another human. Paul's message was that even though one may be a slave in this world, through Christ they are truly free in the Spirit of the Lord. When we accept Jesus Christ as our Lord and Savior, God becomes our master and communicates His will to us through His Spirit.

This does not stop us from sinning. It makes us more aware of our sins. We are, however, forgiven of our sins through faith in Jesus. In addressing this point, Paul tells us about his continual struggle with sin in his letter to the Romans. He tells us that although he wants to do good, there is always the temptation to do something not so good (see Rom.7:21-25). Being saved or born again does not stop us from sinning. We just don't enjoy it anymore. Once you have accepted Jesus as your personal Lord and Savior you begin to feel conviction when you sin, or even think of sinning.

For a believer, wherever there is sin there must also be confession and repentance. If the church ignores or justifies sin by not actively repenting and standing against it, the destructive results become painfully evident in society, filtering down into everyone's daily lives. Addiction is growing at an alarming rate outside of the church, and it also affects many inside its walls. As Christians, we must address these issues in our churches through programs and teachings. This cannot happen if people continue to believe that by accepting Jesus Christ as their Lord and Savior, their battle with addiction will automatically end. If that were the case, it would logically follow that if you tell a lie, or unfairly pass judgment on others, or struggle with bad language, it's evident that you are not saved. Yes, deliverance from addiction can and sometimes does happen because of one's conversion, but that is not the outcome for everyone. We are given the power to overcome and be free, but the process is unique to each individual and according to God's will.

The church is called upon to be the body of Christ who collectively watches over itself, but it has fallen terribly short regarding addiction. The results are becoming more and more evident every year, in society as well as in our own pews. For this reason, I would not suggest consulting a pastor regarding a path to recovery unless that pastor has had significant experience in the field. I have attended AA meetings in churches and heard little to nothing said about Jesus Christ. I believe the reason for this is that many pastors still believe AA is a Christian organization, and since they haven't attended the meetings themselves, they don't realize that in many cases they are not. If a pastor has not had training in how to deal with addiction, I suggest you consider speaking to others who are more qualified.

Above all, do not take these decisions lightly. Addiction is a very serious matter that can lead to serious pain and hardship, not only to the addicts, but to all those who love them. It may seem impossible to do at times, but you must make every attempt to love them through the hardest times and pray for God's strength and deliverance.

10

RELAPSE PREVENTION

I've said it before, but it bears repeating: relapse is not a part of recovery. Relapse is a part of relapse, period. Relapse, for the most part, is rebellion. I'm not talking about someone who tries to quit their addiction on their own and eventually relapses. That kind of relapse signals the need for a formal recovery program. I'm talking about relapse that happens after an addict undergoes some sort of structured program that requires him or her to honestly deal with their issues. Once they have remained abstinent while dealing with the issues that are at the root of their addiction, relapse is a conscious choice to turn in the wrong direction. A relapse can be physically dangerous after a season of sobriety because the body no longer has the previous level of substance present. When people relapse, they tend to return to using their pre-sobriety quantity of the substance. The sudden rush may be more than the body can handle. This may cause serious consequences and complications, including death.

Someone who has never experienced an addiction will probably have a hard time understanding how anyone could ruin their lives once, get help and begin a new, healthy path, only to return to the mess they came from. It does not make logical sense. But addiction is not about intelligence, logic, or common sense. It's about brokenness, and if that brokenness is not dealt with, the chance of relapse is very high.

When the process of recovery focuses on chemicals, psychology, and behavior alone, it only speaks to the intellectual and medical aspects of addiction. Many secular rehabs teach extensively about drugs and how they interact with the body, the psychological causes of addiction, and how changing one's lifestyle and daily behaviors can keep a person from using. As a part of this approach, regular attendance of 12-step meetings is generally required. These meetings provide a constant reminder that an addict is an addict for life. Their remedy for this is attending meetings regularly to maintain sobriety. In these meetings, participants are encouraged to talk about what they're going through, but with one very strict rule. In their opening statement, they are required to recite their first name followed by the words "I am an *alcoholic*," or "I am an *addict*," instilling the belief that once someone is an addict, they will be an addict for life.

This declaration is very helpful in the beginning of the recovery journey. It is essential for someone just starting out to be very aware of their current condition. In secular recovery, a strong case can be made regarding the lifelong struggle that lies ahead. However, in Christian recovery there needs be a point where the addict breaks free of this mentality. Unfortunately, the "once an addict, always an addict" mantra has been around so long even many Christians believe it. How can we believe that Christ died to free us from the ravages of sin and death and believe He cannot or will not free us from addiction? That phrase, "once an addict, always an addict" is a lie from the devil, and it's been very effective. For many in recovery, missing a meeting can bring intense fear and anxiety until they can get "back on track." The meetings become synonymous with sobriety. They believe they cannot stay sober unless they continually go to meetings. Without Christ that may be true, but through Christ there is freedom.

Relapse Prevention

Jesus told us, *"So if the Son sets you free, you are free indeed"* (John 8:36). Paul told us that *"Now the Lord is the Spirit, and where the Spirit of the Lord is, there is freedom"* (2 Cor. 3:17). Accepting Jesus frees us from the grip of sin and death. It does not, however, take away temptation. Everyday life will continue to throw things at us to take us off track. It's no different for an addict than it is for anyone else in that respect. Jesus showed us how to deal with temptation immediately following His baptism. Because He had fasted for forty days, He was extremely vulnerable to temptation by the devil, and the devil took advantage of the opportunity (See Matt. 4:1-11). The devices the devil used to tempt Jesus were the same ones used with Eve in the Garden of Eden, and he has used them on mankind ever since. They were the lust of the eyes, the lust of the flesh and the pride of life (See 1 John 2:16). In Matthew chapter 4, the account of the temptation of Jesus, He speaks out answers to each of the devil's temptations with scripture. Verses 4 and 8, says *"Jesus answered,"* and verse 12 says, *"Jesus said to him."* He spoke out using Scripture to deny the temptation. Once Jesus had made His position clear, the devil departed. This stands as a lesson to all of us as to how we should fight the temptations in our everyday lives.

Just as anyone who did not eat for forty days, Jesus was weak and hungry. Oftentimes, that's how it works: the temptations come when we are at our weakest. Jesus was already armed with knowledge of the Scriptures so He could answer each temptation accordingly. When you are familiar with your weaknesses, you can be prepared for temptations by having knowledge of the specific Scriptures that give you strength. This can only come through prayer and familiarity with Scripture. When you go humbly to the Lord and pray about your weaknesses, He will give you the ammunition you need, should you be tempted in those areas. You may be wondering how you can identify these weaknesses. The Lord will bring that awareness to you in prayer. Whether it's lust, anger, pride, selfishness, envy, jealousy, grief, or anything that is an issue for you, when you have already read and maybe even memorized the verses with which you need to arm yourself, you can act by repeating them out loud when temptation comes.

A discussion about relapse can become very complicated if you entertain the abundance of reasons and excuses that are most often used. The truth is that if someone has had an extended period of time without any substances in their system, relapse is purely a matter of choice. Chemically, there is no longer a reason for the body to be craving the substance, but the person may still crave the escape. Classic examples of this would be longing for a beer during or after a ballgame, or a glass of wine when socializing, or at some other special occasion. Alcohol and marijuana are the most common paths to an addict returning to their drug of choice. A person that was once addicted to heroin, meth, cocaine, MDMA, or some other illegal substance, might convince themselves that having a beer or a glass of wine is not a relapse for them. They know deep down this is not the case, but in the interest of having a drink they will deny what they know to be true. Nearly every time this happens, they return to their drug of choice. It might not happen immediately, but it will eventually happen. Why not have iced tea, soda, fruit punch, water, or some other non-alcoholic beverage? It's because there is a problem with reality that hasn't been addressed, so the desire for escape overrides everything else.

In Christian recovery, the first order of business is to willingly submit to Jesus Christ as your Lord and Savior. Although some believe differently, being saved does not deliver everyone from their addiction without work or effort. I have personally known several people who, after accepting Christ, never desired another drink or drug. They certainly have many other issues in their lives that need to be dealt with, but drugs and alcohol are not among them. For those where this is the case, it was obviously God's will to deliver them from their addiction, but He never eliminates all of our issues at the time of our conversion. It is His prerogative to heal what He heals, as well as choosing when He heals it (See Isa. 55:8-9). The process of regeneration of the entire person, issues and all, is gradual, and God deals with everyone's issues on a personal basis.

When you truly love the Lord, you do not want to do anything you know in your heart will offend Him. If you find yourself being tempted, you can call out to Him for strength and He will answer. The end of the story of Jesus' temptation tells us that angels came and attended to Him. Psalm 91:11 says, *"For He will command His angels concerning you, to guard you in all your ways."* It's not about how strong you are, it's about acknowledging your weakness and calling to the Lord for your strength. His angels are there to guard you, but you must be willing to admit your weakness and submit to His guidance.

What If It Happens

With all of that said and acknowledged, relapse still happens. In the event that you or someone you care about relapses; it is essential to remember that all is not lost. No one loses or forgets all they have experienced and learned just because of a slipup. If a relapse occurs, immediate action is vitally important. For some, every hour after the initial relapse presents more temptation to go further into the black hole that was at one time so familiar. Guilt, shame, disappointment, and even disgust will begin to flood into every thought and emotion. Soon a feeling that all the time spent in recovery is now wasted. This leads to more feelings of worthlessness and hopelessness, which leads to more use. For the addict, it is critical to immediately get to a safe place where there is someone who will keep them away from the substance. If you are a friend or loved one of the addict, keep in mind this is a very unpredictable time. An addict will often choose to go deeper into their addiction before coming back to the reality of needing more help. All you can do is love them, maintain your boundaries, and offer to help them get help when they are ready. It's not the time to show your disappointment in them or be offended that they would go back to what you both know might be a very destructive path. It's a time for love, understanding, forgiveness, and prayer. Simply stand your ground and refuse to help them do anything other than get help from those qualified to give it.

11

REGENERATION: THE HOPE BEYOND REHAB

Rehabilitation is a process that seeks to return someone back to the condition they were in before the affliction. For instance, if a baseball pitcher who has a 90-mph fastball hurts his arm, he will need to go through a rehabilitation process. Once he is again able to throw a 90-mph fastball with the same accuracy, his rehabilitation would be considered complete and successful. I think if we use this definition with regard to addiction, we are missing a very important point. As I have illustrated throughout these pages, addiction is not just about the compulsive use of a substance or the performing of an act. It is more about the brokenness that has led to the behavior more than it is about the behavior itself. Bringing an addict back to the way he or she was before their addiction, meaning sober and broken, will not produce good results. One may stay sober while following the rules of living a sober life, however, what kind of life will he or she have? If they haven't gotten any resolve from the deep issues that caused them to seek an escape, their life of sobriety will never have the deep joy and contentment it could if those issues had been resolved. Even worse, they might end up relapsing into the same addiction, or as many experience, move to a replacement addiction.

Replacing one addiction for another (sometimes called "cross addiction") is quite common, especially when the original addiction was not severe enough to cause a complete breakdown. For instance, I knew a man (Arthur) that had been a functioning alcoholic for many years when he decided to stop drinking after some negative family repercussions and possible health problems arose. He attended a short, outpatient rehab and continued with recovery meetings when the rehab was complete. He also decided to start exercising regularly. He jogged and lifted weights almost every day. In the beginning it seemed like a great plan; he felt better and wasn't drinking anymore, not to mention the weight he lost. He looked and felt great! His working out increased to daily sessions, and ultimately twice daily. He would work out in the morning before work and in the evening on the way home from work. In the beginning of all this his wife was elated. She felt like she had gotten her husband back, and in some ways, even better. His drinking had led to constant arguments and she at one point had even considered divorce. Now he was positive, energetic, and loving. He had started spending time with the children again and their behaviors changed for the better. This lasted for quite a while, until his workout schedule became so time consuming that she started feeling like a single mom. When she confronted him about the time he was spending workout at the expense of his family, his response was that she was never satisfied. She didn't like his drinking and now she didn't like the time he was spending working out. This continued until he hurt himself working out and could no longer jog or lift weights, at least for the foreseeable future. His mood soon became sour about life and the arguing continued, only now it had a different focus. Now he spent all his non-working time at home, and he had become negative and miserable. This lasted for a short while before he began drinking again.

Prior to his injury, one might say that Arthur's rehabilitation was successful in that he not only got back to his previous (before alcoholism) self but had actually become more fit and had a better outlook on life than ever before. Unfortunately, he did not get the healing he needed to be free from his desire to escape. Rehabilitation alone is not the answer. Without healing from the inside out an addict will continually fight with the desire to escape. With willpower and carefully following the rules for behavior change learned in recovery, one may be able to sustain sobriety for many years, even the rest of their life. But without a change of nature, the recovering addict will always have that battle within himself. This is where regeneration comes in.

Regeneration

Regeneration is a term used in Christianity to describe the process of being "born again" in Jesus Christ. The Apostle Paul gives a good description of regeneration as follows: *"Therefore, if anyone is in Christ, the new creation has come: The old has gone, the new is here!"* (2 Cor. 5:17) Whenever a person accepts Jesus Christ as their Lord and Savior, they are changed. It does not necessarily mean they will want to start preaching or become a missionary, but it does mean that God has forgiven them for everything they have done, and their earthly nature has been changed into a heavenly one. The power that is only available through Jesus Christ to live a life of peace and contentment is imparted into every believer regardless of how they have lived their lives up until that point. That does not mean everything instantly becomes good and stays that way. But the inner healing and change that is necessary to be free from the old behaviors becomes available at the time of regeneration. Please don't think I'm saying that if an addict chooses not to be a Christian, he or she cannot live a sober life. I am certainly not saying that. What I am saying is that addiction is an issue that is so individual, so dark, and so deep, that without the help of a Savior, being completely free is nearly, if not completely, impossible.

It is vitally important that as a society we realize the seed of addiction is many, many times planted from a young age. This seed is behavioral, not chemical, making it much harder to identify and treat than if it were only chemical in nature. I have had more than a few people in recovery tell me that one or both of their parents were addicts at one time but had gotten sober either before they were born or shortly after. In speaking with those parents, each time it became disturbingly clear how their child, or sometimes children, became addicts. The parents' views of life, themselves, the world around them, and how they navigate through those things were in many ways the same as an addict, only they were sober. These views and attitudes were passed on to their children and the cycle of addiction continued. The unhealthy ways the parents dealt with life were instilled in their children, leading to the child choosing to escape from reality. They may not have consciously decided to escape, but when they got drunk or high for the first time it introduced the option of taking something to leave the hurt, the confusion, and the unhappy feelings behind, even if it was only for a short time. Sadly, this generational effect, along with the general moral degradation of society, is what is contributing heavily to the current addiction problem we are seeing today.

The Hope that is Beyond Rehab is Jesus Christ. Hope is the assurance that there is something better, something worth striving for, something to get us through the hard times as well as the ability to truly enjoy the good times. As I have said before, some are freed from their addictions at the time they accept Jesus into their hearts. There are others who, after they have been born again, still have a road to travel of learning how to live an addiction free life. It is God's decision as to which path each of us must take. This is true for all of us, not just those struggling with addiction. We all have areas in our lives where we are broken, some more than others. For some their brokenness leads to drug addiction or alcoholism. For others it might be sex addiction, pornography, gambling, or video games. For still others it can lead to over-eating, bitterness, anger, feelings of rejection or abandonment, shame, a poor self-image, or an overblown sense of importance ... the list can go on forever. Regardless of what yours might be, God can provide a way out through His Son Jesus Christ. Whatever path is needed for the best result, trust that God will give you all you need to get through it. He is not only the Hope Beyond Rehab, but also the assurance of all things to come.

12

DRUG INFORMATION

The idea of getting high by ingesting something is practically as old as man himself. I have made it quite clear that my belief is drug addiction is primarily a spiritual issue. In the Bible, we see it mentioned as sorcery. In the Greek it is "pharmakeia" which means the use of medicine, drugs, magic, or spells. This is where we get the English word "pharmacy". One particular biblical reference to this is found in Galatians 5:19-21, where Paul states: *"The acts of the sinful nature are obvious: sexual immorality, impurity and debauchery; idolatry and witchcraft; hatred, discord, jealousy, fits of rage, selfish ambition, dissensions, factions and envy; drunkenness, orgies, and the like. I warn you, as I did before, that those who live like this will not inherit the kingdom of God."* The word translated as "witchcraft" in this verse is the Greek word "pharmakeia". I do not believe it is of much importance that one knows the mechanics, chemistry, or theology behind it except that it is sin of which needs to be confessed and repented. Most of the drugs today are manmade, but that was not always the case. In earlier times man discovered the mind-altering properties of many different plants and combinations of plants which he used to get high or aid in the worship of other gods. Still today in many places combinations of herbs are used for recreational purposes and are the primary avenue to getting high.

Over the past few decades, the scientific community has been doing increasingly more research in the area of addiction. Recently we have seen significant changes in the way the medical and scientific communities have embraced addiction research. Alcoholism seemed to get much more attention after it was considered a disease than when it was just a personal behavioral problem. It is of course much easier to get research money through grants and endowments for a disease than a personal problem. The same goes for drugs. Since the insurance companies have begun to feel pressure to cover the costs of addiction recovery, the pharmaceutical industry has made it a point to introduce drugs to counteract the drugs that are common in the area of addiction. It is much more profitable to have someone take a daily pill that is paid for by their insurance carrier for the rest of their lives than to have them keep taking some street drug (which in many cases is made by the same pharmaceutical company) that may have them committing crimes to feed their addiction. There have been recovery programs springing up nationwide to take advantage of the fact that under our new healthcare laws a greater percentage of the costs of treatment are or will soon be covered, thereby making it a more profitable business. In other words, drug addiction is slowly becoming a lucrative, legitimate business under the disguise of recovery and prevention. This only reinforces my belief that it is a spiritual issue. How else could you possibly explain this greed driven, insane cycle that has otherwise intelligent people so frantically buying into it.

I am certainly not suggesting that all of this research is unnecessary. On the contrary, the more the better as far as I am concerned. The more we know about the physical effects of these drugs, especially after long term use and abuse, the better we can treat those who are damaging their minds and bodies through continued use. What I am saying, however, is if we continue to think we can stop or even slow down drug abuse through tougher laws and more education about the drugs and their effects, we will continue to see more of what has already been happening. Law enforcement will shut down distribution of one drug and another will take its place almost immediately, as in the case of prescription pills and heroin. Law enforcement cracked down heavily on the distribution of prescription pills only to see a sharp increase in heroin addiction and deaths. Many of us in the recovery industry saw this coming from the first mention of more laws being made against prescription meds. It had to happen. Addicts are not going to stop using because they are told to, or because there are stiffer penalties. Nor will cracking down on the distribution of a certain type of drug. They will find whatever means necessary to do whatever they have to do to escape the reality that gives them so much pain. As long as we continue to allow the family unit to drift further from God, we will continue to reap the consequences of the seeds we are sowing.

In the following sections of this chapter, you will find information regarding the more common drugs we deal with in addiction recovery in very unscientific, laymen terms. If you would like to know more about any individual drug regarding its chemical composition or its effects on the mind or body, a quick browser search will yield a plethora of information. Of course, as with anything you research on the internet, do not believe the first couple of things you read. Do a thorough search and study the materials before making any conclusions.

Marijuana

Among the many questions that I ask when interviewing a person for the first time is "how old were you when you first started using?" Almost without fail the first answer will not be when they started using marijuana or drinking alcohol, unless their main issue is alcohol. The first answer will usually be when they started using cocaine, meth, heroin, or some other heavier substance. When I ask a second time, adding that by using I mean marijuana and alcohol as well, the answer will be something like "oh, you mean even smoking pot or drinking beer?" Then the answer is generally years prior to the original answer. This attitude toward marijuana is probably because it does not have as much of a physical addictive component as do other commonly abused drugs. It does however present a real possibility of psychological or emotional dependence, and of course there is the issue of inhaling smoke of any kind being bad for you. It may start as a form of rebellion to societal norms or just another form of what many consider harmless partying, but it becomes much more than that when someone likes the experience and seeks to continue its use.

In recent years the battle to legalize marijuana for recreational use has been raging. There had been a limited amount of research in the effects of marijuana on everyday activities such as driving and child-care, etc., until recently. In the years that I have been interviewing, counseling, and ministering to people that regularly smoked marijuana I have found some very consistent patterns. When someone has been a daily user for more than a few months, they have a harder time processing information during conversations than they do after six months or more of abstinence. Their responses to questions will be quicker and more focused after that period as well. This is not just in a couple of instances. I have found this to be consistent in hundreds of people over the years. It will take many years before the results of any long-term studies can be evaluated. Until then the entire issue of its effects will go back and forth between good and bad with no one really having an unbiased opinion, much less a scientifically provable one. But when we look at it spiritually there is no uncertainty.

As I mentioned earlier, in Scripture we see that drugs can be a form of witchcraft thereby making its use a sin. If you ask a marijuana user why they use it the answer will most often be something like: "it helps me to relax", or "it calms my nerves", or reasons similar to those. The real questions that should be asked are "why do you need something to help you relax after a day at work?", or "what is it that is making you so uptight that you need to take something to relax?" It is the escape from reality that is sought because something about reality is not pleasant. If your reality was enjoyable there would be no reason to seek a way out of it, especially if it costs increasingly more money to achieve the desired effect because of your increasing tolerance.

Marijuana does not have nearly the withdrawal symptoms as most other drugs or alcohol. If someone has been using daily for an extended period, they may experience some anxiety or uneasiness. As in all cases of doing or taking something regularly, the effects of quitting can vary from one person to another. However, the reason for using it does not go away because of using it, meaning that if you are using it to help you relax you will have a hard time relaxing without it for a while. How long depends on the individual and their level of issues leading to its use. The root issues that created the need to escape must be examined and dealt with eventually or the use will continue, or worse, become compulsive. It may eventually shift to something stronger and more addictive, thus causing more damage to the mind, body, and soul.

Synthetic Marijuana

Synthetic marijuana has become quite popular in recent years especially among teenagers and young adults. One of the main attractions to these types of drugs is that they are cheap, and in many cases, legal. Although they are not as popular as marijuana itself, there has been an alarming increase of use among young people. Although there have been over one hundred different variations found so far, there are two main families or categories that these drugs fall into. One is "synthetic cannabinoid", which is the closest to marijuana. The other is "synthetic cathinone", which is similar to amphetamines (stimulants). They are called a variety of names, some of which are K2, Spice, Bath Salts, Potpourri, even Jewelry Cleaner. This is far from a complete list since there are numerous street names and slangs used by those who buy and use them, and new names are made up regularly. These drugs are generally manufactured by spraying chemicals onto some sort of plant so that it can be smoked. They are extremely dangerous, especially since you never know what ingredients went into making them. There is no commonality from one kind or brand to another and in many cases the ingredients used in their production are legal, so many of them can be sold in the corner store. Government agencies are continually updating laws in an attempt to get some control over their distribution, but it is an uphill battle. It seems that the ingredients are changing faster than they can outlaw them.

The immediate effects of these drugs can vary and are quite unpredictable given the fact that every batch can contain a different combination of ingredients. A few years ago, there was a man from Miami who, after taking bath salts, ate a homeless person's face until he was killed by police. Although this type of behavior is not common, this and similar events have taken place which should give pause to anyone considering their use. The more common effects can include seizures, racing heartbeat, high blood pressure, anxiety, nausea and vomiting, chest pain, hallucinations, extreme paranoia, violent outbursts, and suicidal thoughts or actions.

I had one experience with a man on K2 who was completely unaware of his surroundings and unresponsive to any conversation, appearing unable to talk. He remained in that state for at least two hours before walking off like a zombie. I have not seen him since. There have been numerous deaths attributed to these drugs as well as psychotic episodes, the effects of which have been known to have some long-term residual effects. Permanent brain damage is certainly a possibility, even with only one use. These drugs are extremely dangerous. If you know someone who is using this type of drug, it would be wise to either convince them to get help or protect yourself from them should they become violent or incoherent.

Medical Marijuana

I will start by saying I am not a physician or medical professional. The use of medical marijuana warrants serious consideration if suggested by a doctor. Whether medical marijuana (aka medical cannabis) is a good thing or not has been a hot topic for many years. I do not think that smoking it for any reason is a good idea. Fortunately, smoking is unnecessary with medical marijuana, so that is not an issue. They center the debate on whether it is safer and more effective than prescription drugs already available for the condition being treated. There are strong opinions on both sides of the debate about whether it should treat a growing number of medical conditions. I know several people who have been taking it as prescribed by their doctors with positive results. That being said, I do not agree with its use in most cases.

Where it is legal, it does not differ from any other drug prescribed by a medical professional. In one sense, that is a good thing. In another, it is not. On the positive side, once it has been determined to be the best treatment for a condition, then it should be easily obtainable. On the negative side, I have seen addicts manipulate their doctors into believing they need it. Many addicts did the same with opiates for a long time. By "doctor shopping", the process of visiting different doctors until you find one who will prescribe what you want, you could feed your addiction legally. To make it even easier, "pill mills" began cropping up. These are medical centers set up by certain unethical doctors where one could seek treatment for some chronic problem such as "back pain" and walk out with an opiate prescription. These "clinics" became quite popular in the addiction community. Federal and state governments dealt this practice a death blow through tightening regulations on pharmacies and doctors resulting in raids and arrests across the country. I had one client tell me that while he was sitting in jail for a drug possession charge, he was amused to see his doctor walk in dressed in a jail issued jumpsuit. It's easy to understand his amusement.

You might ask how this relates to the medical marijuana issue. It is very much the same. There are doctors who have become known for their willingness to prescribe marijuana. Addicts know they can get medical marijuana cards, making it much safer to purchase and use. Since most people in the US assume that marijuana is beneficial and even non-addictive, this easy access does not appear to be a problem. My years of one-on-one experience with regular users has proven otherwise, but that is beyond this book. I suggest that anyone considering long-term use, medical or otherwise, does some research. The results may shock you.

Ecstasy

One of the more commonly known synthetic drugs is ecstasy, also known as MDMA. It produces effects closely associated with two other drugs, meth, and mescaline. It can produce a stimulant effect much like methamphetamines, and the hallucinogenic effects of mescaline (a psychedelic drug similar to LSD). It is most commonly taken in pill form; however, it can also be found in powder form which is generally snorted (inhaled). Ecstasy gives a euphoric experience while distorting one's perception of time and space. Extreme sensitivity to being touched, causing an overwhelmingly pleasurable response is also a common effect. It is commonly "cut" (combined with another substance primarily to increase profits) with other substances which adds to the danger of its use. In many cases, MDMA is cut with other stimulants such as cocaine, caffeine, methamphetamines, DXM (a drug found in some cough syrups that can create a feeling of being high), and even ketamine, which is an anesthetic used in treating animals.

The immediate dangers of using this drug are much the same as any other stimulant. These can include strain on the heart, increased blood pressure, and racing, confusing thoughts. These effects will many times result in increased sensitivity to fear and present a potential for overreacting to environmental conditions. There is also the possibility of a sudden increase in body temperature which can result in internal organ damage and even organ failure.

The after-effects of using ecstasy may include problems sleeping, depression, and severe anxiety. These effects can last anywhere from days to weeks, depending on the individual and duration of regular use prior to abstinence. Withdrawal after continued use is not as painful or potentially dangerous as alcohol or opiates (heroin), but the effects can last much longer than most other substances after use is discontinued.

Flakka

This drug is very dangerous!! It has not become very popular, and I only included it here because of how dangerous it can be with as little as one use. It has popped up over the past few years and has cause some pretty severe problems for many who have used it. It is a synthetic stimulant that can be ingested by snorting, eating, smoking, or even vaping in an e-cigarette. It is sometimes called "gravel" because of its appearance. It comes in the form of small cloudy crystals that can be ground into a powder for snorting or shooting, or just swallowed whole if that is one's preference. It causes the body temperature to rise to over 104 degrees which many times results in the user taking off their clothes. It also gives them amazing strength, much like a super adrenaline rush, and causes psychotic behavior. There are eyewitness accounts of people running naked down city streets, jumping out of windows, slamming themselves against walls, and even one instance of a man breaking into a police station by going through the front window. It has been known to take four or five police officers to subdue one man under the influence of flakka. I can honestly say this is not something I would ever want to experience or even witness.

There are other less popular synthetic drugs available on the street, but I think you have the idea by now. They are very, very dangerous and the effects are for the most part unpredictable.

Prescription Medications

Many children grow up watching their parents take a pill for literally every ache and pain they have. They hear mom say to her friend jokingly that she needs to take a pill to chill out, only the child sees her take the pill when they get home. When the child gets a runny nose, or a bump on the head out come the pills. We have taught our children that the answer to any discomfort is taking a pill. Now we are paying the price for that foolishness. Children are starting to abuse pills of varying types at a younger age than ever before. They have little or no fear of what the results of taking unneeded medication can be. From a child's perspective, taking a pill to make discomfort go away is perfectly acceptable, even when the discomfort is minimal at best.

There are many prescription medications that lend themselves to abuse and have become quite popular recently. Medications for sleep, pain, anxiety, and depression are among the most abused. That is not to say that others cannot be abused, those are simply the ones that are abused the most. Until recently, opiate-based prescription pain medications have been the most serious problem from the law enforcement standpoint. For the past decade there has been a big push by law enforcement agencies to crack down on the distribution of these pain medications. These efforts have been successful in one sense and disturbing in another. The pills have been harder to get on the street so the price per pill has gone up. This has given an opening for the heroin distributors to take advantage of the situation by flooding the streets with heroin at ridiculously low prices. When the dealers began pushing the pill takers to try heroin instead of the more expensive pills, it resulted in a sharp increase of heroin use which has reached epidemic proportions.

It has become common for children to steal pills from their parents' medicine cabinets, purses, glove boxes, etc., take them to school and use them with their friends. There have been reports of parties where each child brings as many pills as they can safely steal from home, put them in a hat and take turns reaching in to pull out as many as they can hold. Then, they either take all the pills at once or periodically as the party progresses. Most of the time they do not even know what it is they are taking.

There are some unfortunate long-term effects of addiction to pain medications that are carried into sobriety. One being that, if at any time in the future pain medication is needed for a legitimate reason, such as dental work, broken bones, surgery, etc., the addiction may be reignited causing abuse of the drug. The same withdrawal symptoms experienced at the beginning of your sobriety might also be an issue. Although this is not always the case, it is quite common. We sometimes call this "waking up the monster." If the inner issues that were at the root of your addiction were dealt with completely during recovery, chances are you will only need a short detox period to end the cravings. It is also common for opiate addicts, whether in recovery or throughout their lives after recovery, to have an increased tolerance for pain medications. It will require much more of the drug to relieve their pain than what the doctors are willing to allow. There are non-narcotic pain medications available, but they are not very effective in treating high levels of pain. This is something that just about every opiate addict who has successfully gone through recovery will have to deal with if they are ever in a position of needing pain relief.

Heroin

Heroin is extremely addictive and devastating to the mind and body. It can be snorted or injected. It is very common for someone to begin heroin use by snorting it, especially if they have an aversion to needles. It does not take long for the user to begin injecting it once the drug has lowered their inhibitions. Injection provides the user with a quicker, more intense high. Once it is snorted the perceived need for more becomes quite overpowering. In most of the people that I have discussed this with, a person uses heroin for the first time with someone that is already using it. Once the first timer has snorted it and wants more, the suggestion is made to "shoot" it, with the experienced one offering to help. Because the newbie is high, whatever common sense or restraint that may have existed is gone and using a needle seems like a better way of continuing the experience, even if they are normally scared to death of needles. This brings up another danger of using this and many other drugs, needles.

A person that is getting high is not very concerned with the dangers of their using while they are high. Even if a person is normally very cautious about hygiene and overall cleanliness, once they are high it all goes out the window. Sharing needles or using a needle that may have been used previously is something that can have serious repercussions. HIV and Hepatitis are just two of the viruses that can be transferred by sharing needles. Anyone that has been using drugs intravenously should be screened for both of these at the very least.

Heroin is an opiate, a substance that is also used in prescription pain medications, which have become the drug of choice for many addicts. Recently, law enforcement around the country began shutting down the supply of opiate based prescription pain medications. Because of this, the availability has gone down, and the price has increased on the streets. As of this writing, it costs thirty dollars for one opiate pill on the streets and five dollars for a small bag of heroin. Naturally the heroin wins out producing a flood of new heroin addicts who used to be pill addicts. From the perspective of someone that does not understand drugs or addiction it might look as though there is little difference. After all, heroin and pain pills are both opiates. The difference is that the pills are manufactured by pharmaceutical companies and are regulated for quality and contents. Heroin does not have these controls. It is not sold to the end user in its pure state. It is mixed with other substances in order to diminish its potency and increase its profit margin. There is no way to know what the dealer has used to cut the heroin, so there is a real danger of overdose or death. There has been a continual rise in heroin related deaths, and most recently the deaths have been the result of heroin mixed with fentanyl. I cover fentanyl in the next section.

Heroin is a very difficult drug to stop using. The detox process is painful and can sometimes be frightening. If someone has been using heroin for an extended period of time, their tolerance for pain is probably quite low, so any amount of pain seems unbearable. This makes the process of quitting quite unpleasant, at least for a while. Detoxification, which generally takes between seven to ten days, should be done in a medical facility familiar with the process. Detox should be followed by immediate entry into a recovery program.

Fentanyl

Fentanyl is a synthetically produced opioid. It is reported to be up to 100 times stronger than morphine and 50 times stronger than heroin. It was developed for pain management and is also used in conjunction with other drugs for anesthesia. On the street, it is commonly mixed with heroin, cocaine, or methamphetamines to increase the effects of those drugs. Because of the potency of the drug, only a small amount is needed to produce an intense high. By mixing a small amount of fentanyl with other drugs, the resulting high is much greater than without it. This allows the dealer to use less of the more expensive drug, such as heroin or cocaine, and more cutting substance such as baking soda, sugar, starch or even rat poison. By adding a small amount of fentanyl, the resulting high will be more pronounced. This causes the user to desire the fentanyl laced product above the others. From the dealer's perspective, it is a win-win. The customer gets what they want, and the dealer makes a bigger profit.

There are some problems with this, however. One being that the fentanyl used by the dealer is probably what is known as "illicitly manufactured fentanyl." It can be obtained in both powered and liquid form. Because of its incredible potency, a very small amount may cause death by overdose. In addition, it does not change the smell or taste of the original substance to which it is added. This makes it impossible for the user to know in advance if they are about to ingest it. It has been reported by multiple news outlets and government agencies that the number of overdose deaths due to fentanyl from April 2020 through April 2021 was over one hundred thousand. This is the highest number of overdoses ever recorded in one year. I have personally known several people who have died using this drug, the oldest of them being under forty years of age. It is a very dangerous drug when used by anyone other than a medical professional specifically trained for its use.

Cocaine

Cocaine is an incredibly addictive stimulant drug. It can be obtained in two forms, powdered and crack (a free-based form or cocaine that has the appearance of small, jagged rocks).

Because cocaine is a stimulant, in many instances it is used in conjunction with alcohol. Alcohol is a depressant which means it can bring a drinker down once the initial effects wear off, so cocaine is sometimes used by alcoholics to get going again. The opposite is also common where the user has used enough cocaine to become extremely anxious and uses alcohol or marijuana to calm down.

The powder is generally snorted but it is sometimes wiped on the gums. The powder when snorted is extremely harmful to the nasal passages. In cases of long-term usage, the nasal passages may be destroyed requiring surgery. It is also sometimes mixed with heroin resulting in a different kind of high than either one provides on its own. This combination increases the chances of overdose, especially since both are usually "cut", (combined with other substances such as another drug, laxative, or baking powder), and the user generally does not know what was used to cut it, nor how much it was cut.

Crack cocaine is a crystalized rock that is heated and smoked. It is extremely addictive. It is generally smoked in a pipe, or a makeshift device made out of aluminum foil, or an empty beverage can. One hit of crack can easily begin a binge that may last hours, days, weeks, or even months. This usually depends on the availability of the crack and the money needed to purchase it. I once had a client who, together with his girlfriend, had been on a three-month binge spending close to a quarter of a million dollars. The intense desire for more that comes shortly after the last use can cause the user to do things they would never have previously considered. There is a loss of appetite and quick weight loss when using cocaine, especially crack. Many crimes and acts of violence result from this drug every year. This can be attributed both to the intensity of the high as well as the uncontrollably urgent desire for more. This desire will often cause the user to violate his own morals and character resulting in things such as stealing from parents or loved ones, or burglary to get the money needed for the next high.

Cocaine can be extremely difficult to stop using, although its detox intensity is not nearly as severe as opiates or alcohol. It is important to note that even after long periods of sobriety the addiction can be back in full swing with one use. There are several different drugs that are used to help an addict stop using cocaine, but it is really no different than any other drug as far as recovery is concerned. If the deep issues that keep a person running from reality are addressed and there is a change of heart, the addiction no longer has anything to feed. Then getting high will no longer be an option for relief or escape from whatever life has in store for them.

Meth (Methamphetamines)

Meth is short for methamphetamine. It is sometimes referred to as "speed". It can be used by snorting, smoking, injecting, or taken orally. It also comes in another form known as "crystal meth". Street names can include "ice", "glass", or "crank", among others. In this form its appearance is much like small chunks of ice. Crystal meth is generally smoked, much like crack cocaine. It can be manufactured using over-the-counter ingredients which are relatively inexpensive. The quickest and most intense high comes from smoking or injection and lasts only a short time, sometimes as little as a few minutes. Taking it orally or snorting it takes longer for the effect to kick in and the high is not as intense as experienced through injection.

The physical toll that this drug takes on the user is significant. Loss of teeth, dehydration, loss of hair, and mental and nervous system disorders are not uncommon among regular users. In addition, skin irritations and sores can develop along with the appearance of being much older than one's chronological age.

Withdrawal symptoms can include intense cravings for the drug, anxiety, depression, sleeplessness, and severe fatigue. The physical and mental effects of meth can sometimes reverse themselves over time, but not in all cases.

Anti-Drug Drugs

There has recently been an increase of research done in the area of medications that can be used to help the recovery process. Some recovery programs include these medications as part of their treatment. It is sometimes referred to as "Evidence Based Medication Therapy". Medications used in this process can include buprenorphine (known as Subutex in sublingual form), suboxone (a buprenorphine and naloxone combination), methadone, and naltrexone (Vivitrol). This is not a complete list; however, these have proven to be most popular recently. They can only be obtained with a doctor's prescription. I cannot say that I am a fan of this method of recovery. The idea of establishing a regimen of taking one medication to aid in abstaining from another tends to defy reasoning. I have seen some studies that claim these replacement drugs can sometimes lessen the severity of withdrawal, especially in the case of opiates, but I personally have yet to talk with anyone that has had that result. In my experience with people who have taken these replacement drugs, the withdrawal from the new drug is just as painful as the original addictive substance it was supposed to replace. What this approach does seem to do is give the treatment facility, judicial system, or a physician control over a person's usage through carefully monitored distribution and dosage. If that is the motivation behind this practice it is working, however, without treatment the person will never be able to function normally.

This approach may take care of the street purchase problem, but if it is not used in conjunction with a program of strict accountability and care targeting the addict's core issues, it only serves to extend the person's addiction. For example, I have had numerous clients who have been on some form of medication therapy for extended periods of time only to relapse when the replacement drug dosage is lowered or discontinued. The reason for this is the cravings and severe sickness that were supposed to be avoided through the medication therapy were only delayed until the replacement drug was discontinued. The resulting discomfort from the absence of the replacement drug then leads to relapse (usually to the original drug) to relieve the pain of withdrawal.

As an example, methadone (mentioned above) is used to help control and hopefully alleviate an opiate addict's addiction. It is generally dispersed daily at a clinic where the addict can stop by to receive their daily dose and go on with their normal activities. Visiting a clinic that distributes the daily doses of methadone can be alarming. Prior to opening in the morning there is usually a line of people waiting for their daily dose. Many of those waiting will have an extremely unhealthy look about them. After they take their prescribed dosage, they can then go about their day, even though when taking these medications, they continue to demonstrate the same mannerisms characteristic of an addict when they are high. The lethargic, glassy eyed appearance coupled with little or no motivation in their everyday lives will remain until they are completely clean of all substances.

There are currently groups and organizations lobbying for the government to establish provisions for clinics and facilities that provide this type of treatment. I cannot agree with this line of action because it does not put the focus on the issues that cause the addiction. It is always stated that there should be counseling and group participation while taking the alternative drugs in hope of eventually discontinuing it. This might sound good and even make sense, however, once the replacement drug has been taken for a short time, the individual becomes addicted to the replacement. The pain of detoxing off the replacements is sometimes worse than it is with the original opiate. In our facility we encounter many who have gone through this type of program only to seek help getting clean from the therapy medications. Here is an example of what I have experienced in helping those faced with this situation. This scenario has played out the same from person to person, with few exceptions.

One dangerous misconception regarding these medications is that once a person is taking them, they are clean. In drug addicts' lingo this means they are no longer taking their drug of choice. I have had many people interview for entry into our program claiming to have been "clean" for weeks, only to find out they have been taking one of the recovery drugs. Experience has taught me that even after decreasing their doses over a long period of time, when they finally discontinue their use, withdrawal can be quite severe. Without exception, every time the "clean" person was admitted for recovery, another admission to a detox facility was necessary before a recovery plan could be initiated.

A Final Word

There are many more drugs and addictive substances than what I have covered here. These are, in my opinion, the most common. There is an endless supply of information on the internet about the drugs listed here, as well as any others that might interest you. An important thing to remember is that it is not so much the drug or activity that one is addicted to as it is the reason for the addiction itself. The intent of this book is to give you a basic overview of drugs, drug addiction, and alcoholism from the perspective of someone who has worked with addicts and alcoholics in recovery for many years. My goal is to help guide you in making informed decisions regarding recovery options when dealing with someone in your life that needs help. It is much more important to show you care about someone struggling with addiction than it is to lecture them on the dangers of the substances they are abusing. Chances are they already know more about the drug than you do but have yet to have someone care enough to see them through the process of getting the help they need.

Drug Information

There is one thing I have found to be more important than any other aspect of recovery. Belief and trust in God through Jesus Christ. That, above all else, can bring freedom from drugs, alcohol, pornography, gambling, and any other life-altering challenges one might encounter.

13

BEFORE YOU GO

I truly hope you have found answers in these pages. If you think there is something here that others might benefit from knowing, **please let them know by leaving a brief review on whatever platform you chose to purchase this book.** It only takes a minute and will help others who are looking for guidance and options for their loved ones.

There are many who are suffering, and many who are looking on with broken hearts wanting to help but not knowing where to begin. Please share the information you have gathered from these pages so someone else may benefit from your effort in reading them. Thank you for taking the time to do this. I really appreciate your support. God bless.

ABOUT THE AUTHOR

CHARLES CAMORATA is the Pastor of Open Homes Fellowship Church and Director of the Open Homes Fellowship Drug and Alcohol Recovery Program, a Christian residential program for men struggling with drug and alcohol addiction. He resides in Orlando, Florida.

For more information, please visit:
www.HopeBeyondRehab.com

For information regarding the Open Homes Fellowship Program, please visit:
www.OpenHomesFellowship.org

Made in the USA
Las Vegas, NV
14 June 2023